LEADERSHIP FOR WOMEN

BUILD CONFIDENCE, COMMUNICATE WITH IMPACT
AND LEAD WITH PURPOSE IN YOUR CAREER,
BUSINESS AND LIFE

FREEDOM PUBLICATIONS

Copyright © 2025 Freedom Publications. All rights reserved.

The content within this book may not be reproduced, duplicated, or transmitted without direct written permission from the author or the publisher.

Under no circumstances will any blame or legal responsibility be held against the publisher, or author, for any damages, reparation, or monetary loss due to the information contained within this book, either directly or indirectly.

Legal Notice:

This book is copyright protected. It is only for personal use. You cannot amend, distribute, sell, use, quote, or paraphrase any part of the content within this book, without the consent of the author or publisher.

Disclaimer Notice:

Please note the information contained within this document is for educational and entertainment purposes only. All effort has been expended to present accurate, up-to-date, reliable, and complete information. No warranties of any kind are declared or implied. Readers acknowledge that the author is not engaged in the rendering of legal, financial, medical, or professional advice. The content within this book has been derived from various sources. Please consult a licensed professional before attempting any techniques outlined in this book.

By reading this document, the reader agrees that under no circumstances is the author responsible for any losses, direct or indirect, that are incurred as a result of the use of the information contained within this document, including, but not limited to, errors, omissions, or inaccuracies.

CONTENTS

Introduction ... 7

1. FOUNDATIONS OF AUTHENTIC CONFIDENCE ... 11
   Understanding Your Unique Leadership Style ... 12
   Overcoming Self-Doubt in Male-Dominated Industries ... 14
   Confidence-Building Exercises for Everyday Leadership ... 17
   Building a Supportive Inner Dialogue ... 19

2. MASTERING ASSERTIVE COMMUNICATION ... 23
   Breaking Down Barriers to Assertive Communication ... 23
   Techniques for Being Heard Without Being Perceived Negatively ... 26
   Developing Your Executive Presence ... 28
   Navigating Difficult Conversations with Confidence ... 31

3. LEVERAGING MENTORSHIP AND NETWORKING ... 35
   Identifying and Approaching the Right Mentor ... 35
   Building Your Networking Ninja Skills ... 37
   Creating a Circle of Influence ... 40
   Leveraging Professional Networks for Career Advancement ... 43

4. NAVIGATING GENDER BIAS AND WORKPLACE CHALLENGES ... 47
   Understanding and Combating Gender Bias ... 47
   Strategies for Gaining Visibility and Recognition ... 49
   Overcoming Imposter Syndrome ... 52
   Balancing Professional Ambitions with Personal Life ... 54

5. CRAFTING YOUR PERSONAL BRAND ... 59
   Defining Your Personal Brand ... 59
   Increasing Your Visibility in the Workplace ... 62
   Personal Branding Techniques for Career Growth ... 64
   Aligning Your Brand with Your Leadership Style ... 67

6. ENHANCING EMOTIONAL INTELLIGENCE AND
   SELF-AWARENESS   71
   Understanding the Role of Emotional Intelligence in
   Leadership   71
   Exercises for Enhancing Self-Awareness   74
   Empathy Mapping for Effective Leadership   77
   Decision-Making with Emotional Intelligence   79

7. RESILIENCE AND ADAPTABILITY IN
   LEADERSHIP   85
   Building Resilience: Bouncing Back from Setbacks   85
   Developing Adaptability in Dynamic Environments   87
   Leading Through Uncertainty and Change   90
   Strategies for Sustaining Momentum During
   Challenges   92

8. INCLUSIVE LEADERSHIP AND DIVERSITY   97
   Embracing Diverse Leadership Styles   97
   Fostering an Inclusive Work Environment   100
   The Role of Diversity in Innovation and Growth   102
   Leading with Empathy and Understanding   105

9. GOAL SETTING AND ACHIEVING SUCCESS   109
   Vision Casting for Personal and Professional Success   109
   Setting SMART Goals for Leadership Growth   111
   Aligning Goals with Personal Values   114
   Creating a Strategic Plan for Success   117

10. COMMUNICATION TECHNIQUES FOR IMPACT   121
    Mastering Public Speaking and Presentation Skills   121
    The Art of Persuasion and Influence   123
    Using Digital Communication Tools Effectively   126
    Building Rapport and Trust in Teams   129

11. WORK-LIFE INTEGRATION STRATEGIES   133
    Understanding Work-Life Integration vs. Balance   133
    Techniques for Managing Stress and Preventing
    Burnout   136
    Creating Boundaries That Protect Personal Time   138
    Integrating Personal Well-being into Leadership   141

12. INSPIRING ACTION AND LEADING WITH
    PURPOSE 145
    Cultivating a Growth Mindset for Leadership 145
    Inspiring and Motivating Your Team 148
    Leading with Authenticity and Integrity 150
    Sustaining Purpose-Driven Leadership: An In-Depth
    Exploration 153

Conclusion 157
References 163
About the Publisher 167

INTRODUCTION

In a bustling conference room, Sarah sat at the table, surrounded by her male colleagues. She had prepared for this meeting for weeks, confident in her ideas and ready to share them. Yet, as the conversation flowed, she found herself hesitating, her voice drowned out by louder ones. It wasn't just the noise that silenced her, it was the doubt that crept in, whispering that her ideas weren't valuable enough. Sarah's story is not unique. Many women find themselves in similar situations, feeling unheard and undervalued, despite their abilities.

This book aims to change that narrative. It is a guide to empower you, to help you embrace your unique strengths and lead with authenticity in your career, business, and life. The purpose here is simple yet profound: to give you the tools and mindset to lead as your true self, without compromise.

Women often face unique challenges in leadership. Confidence issues, communication barriers, and navigating gender bias are just a few. These challenges can hold you back from reaching your potential and can make leadership feel like an uphill battle. But these are not insurmountable obstacles. This book presents actionable solutions to these problems, offering a path forward.

By reading this book, you can expect to build your confidence and improve your communication skills. You'll develop a leadership mindset rooted in self-awareness and purpose. You'll learn to navigate the complexities of leadership with clarity and strength. These are not just skills for the workplace, they are skills for life.

At Freedom Publications, we have always been passionate about leadership and the unique role women play in it. In my early career, I faced many of the same challenges you might be experiencing. There were moments of doubt and uncertainty, but there were also moments of incredible growth. These experiences taught me valuable lessons about resilience and authenticity. They inspired me to help other women overcome similar hurdles, to see that they, too, can lead with confidence and purpose.

The structure of this book is designed to guide you on your journey. Each chapter focuses on a key aspect of leadership for women. We'll start with building authentic confidence, exploring practical strategies to overcome self-doubt. Next, we'll dive into effective communication, helping you find your voice in any setting. We'll tackle imposter syndrome and the importance of setting healthy boundaries. Decision-making, delegation, and leading with emotional intelligence will also be explored. Throughout, we'll develop a leadership mindset that aligns with your values and vision.

I invite you to fully engage with this book. Reflect on the stories and strategies shared, and consider how they apply to your own life. Take the exercises seriously, and use them as a springboard for change. You have the power to transform your leadership approach and make a meaningful impact in your career and beyond.

The key takeaway of the book is this: You don't necessarily need to change who you are to lead. You just need the proper support and strategies to lead as your true self. This journey is about transformation, about growing into the leader you were always meant to be. As you explore the strategies within this book, I hope you find inspiration and empowerment.

1

FOUNDATIONS OF AUTHENTIC CONFIDENCE

Let's begin by exploring what it means to lead with confidence, communicate with impact, and live with purpose. The moment I realized the power of confidence was not an earth-shattering epiphany but a quiet recognition, I was sitting in a small meeting room, surrounded by decision-makers who seemed to carry their weight with ease. I, on the other hand, felt like an imposter. My ideas were solid, but I hesitated, wondering if they would be well received or if I would be dismissed. That hesitation was my enemy, and it took time to see that confidence was not about being the loudest or most assertive voice in the room. It was about trusting my voice and knowing it had worth. You might have felt this too, a moment when you doubted your place or your worth. But understanding and embracing your unique leadership style can change that narrative.

UNDERSTANDING YOUR UNIQUE LEADERSHIP STYLE

Leadership is not a one-size-fits-all concept. It's a dynamic and evolving skill that reflects who you are at your core. Identifying your unique leadership style is vital because it helps you lead in a way that feels genuine and effective. This self-awareness boosts your confidence because you're not trying to fit into a mold that doesn't suit you. Instead, you're leveraging your natural strengths.

Leadership style assessments can be instrumental in this process. They offer insights into your personality traits, strengths, and areas for growth. These assessments are not about labeling you but about highlighting the unique qualities you bring to the table. Whether you align with a transformational style, inspiring and motivating others by creating a vision for the future, or a servant leadership approach, focusing on the growth and well-being of your team, these insights can be empowering (Predictive Index). By embracing these styles, you can navigate situations more effectively, knowing how best to apply your strengths.

But understanding your leadership style is just one piece of the puzzle. It's crucial to align this style with your personal values. Leadership becomes most effective when it resonates with what you truly believe in. Consider leaders who prioritize ethical practices and transparency because honesty is a core value for them. Their teams often follow suit, fostering a culture of trust and integrity. Similarly, when your actions as a leader reflect your values, authenticity naturally follows.

To illustrate this, let's look at leaders who have succeeded by staying true to their values. Consider Nelson Mandela, whose leadership was deeply rooted in justice and equality (Harvard Kennedy School). His commitment to these principles inspired movements and brought about significant change, showing that value-driven leadership can have profound impacts.

Self-awareness is the bedrock of understanding both your leadership style and values. It involves recognizing your strengths and areas for growth, which can be achieved through self-reflection exercises and personal SWOT analyses. By identifying these facets within yourself, your Strengths, Weaknesses, Opportunities, and Threats (SWOT), you gain clarity on where you excel and where you need improvement.

Self-Reflection Exercise: Personal SWOT Analysis

- *Strengths:* What are you naturally good at? Which skills or traits have others consistently praised?
- *Weaknesses:* What challenges do you face regularly? Where do you feel less confident?
- *Opportunities:* What external factors could you leverage to enhance your leadership?
- *Threats:* What obstacles stand in your way of achieving success?

This exercise is a starting point for deeper introspection and ongoing growth.

Embracing individuality in leadership means recognizing that no one else has your unique combination of experiences and perspectives. This individuality is not something to hide, it's something to celebrate. Maximize your personal strengths by aligning them with your leadership roles. If you're a great listener, use this skill to understand team dynamics better and foster open communication. If you're innovative, lead initiatives that encourage creative problem-solving.

Your personal brand should reflect this individuality. It's not just about how others perceive you, but how you present yourself consistently across all platforms, social media, meetings, or even casual interactions. Aligning your brand with your leadership style ensures that people see the real you, someone who leads by example and remains true to their values.

Confidence in leadership stems from authenticity. When you lead as yourself without wearing a mask or conforming to others' expectations, you naturally exude confidence. So, as you explore these strategies and insights throughout the book, remember that each step you take towards understanding and embracing your unique leadership style is a step towards leading with true confidence.

OVERCOMING SELF-DOUBT IN MALE-DOMINATED INDUSTRIES

In these environments where male voices often dominate, self-doubt can creep in subtly yet persistently. It might start as a whisper questioning your presence in the room, whether your contributions are as valuable or if your voice even matters. This doubt is not born from a lack of ability but from societal expectations and entrenched gender norms that have long dictated whose voices are heard. From a young age, many women are subtly encouraged to defer to male authority, to be agreeable rather than assertive. Over time, these expectations shape how you perceive your capabilities, often undermining your confidence in professional settings.

Combatting this internalized doubt requires intentional strategies. Positive affirmations can be remarkably powerful in shifting your mindset. By consistently affirming your strengths and worth, you gradually rewire your brain to focus on your capabilities rather than imagined inadequacies. Consider starting each day with a simple affirmation: "I am competent and my ideas are valuable." Repeated over time, these words can replace doubt with certainty.

Mindfulness and grounding exercises also play a crucial role in managing self-doubt. In moments of anxiety or uncertainty, pause to take slow, deliberate breaths. Focus on the sensation of air filling your lungs and grounding you in the present moment. This practice helps break the cycle of negative thoughts, bringing clarity and calmness. It reminds you that your presence is not only valid but necessary.

The stories of women who have triumphed over self-doubt offer both inspiration and practical insights. Take for instance the narrative of a female executive who once struggled with her confidence in board meetings dominated by men. Through interviews, she shared that she initially felt out of place, her voice overshadowed by colleagues who seemed more confident. However, she chose to focus on preparation and knowledge, ensuring she was the most informed person in the room. Her meticulous preparation built her credibility, earning her the respect of peers and boosting her confidence.

Such narratives illuminate the path forward. They demonstrate that perseverance and self-belief can transform doubt into determination. A structured framework for continuous confidence-building further supports this transformation. Participating in confidence-building workshops can provide practical tools, and peer support groups offer a safe space to share experiences and strategies. These groups connect you with others facing similar challenges, helping you realize that you are not alone in this struggle.

Confidence-Building Workshops

Consider attending workshops that focus on public speaking or negotiation skills, areas where confidence often falters. These workshops offer a supportive environment to practice and refine these skills without judgment. Engaging with peers who understand your experiences fosters a sense of community and shared growth.

Peer support groups play an equally vital role. These gatherings are not just about sharing stories, they are about creating a network of encouragement and accountability. They provide a platform where you can discuss setbacks and celebrate successes without fear of judgment.

A continuous commitment to building confidence is essential. This isn't a one-time effort but an ongoing process, where each small win contributes to a larger tapestry of self-assuredness. The framework for developing this confidence includes setting realistic goals, celebrating achievements, and seeking feedback from trusted mentors who understand your journey.

In male-dominated settings where doubt can easily overshadow ambition, these strategies enable you to reclaim your space and voice. It is not just about overcoming doubt but about embracing your capabilities and potential fully. The work you do on yourself reflects outwardly, influencing how others perceive and interact with you.

By implementing these techniques and drawing inspiration from those who've walked this path before, you can counteract self-doubt effectively. The key lies in acknowledging that while societal norms may have shaped initial perceptions, they do not define your abilities or worth. The power to redefine these narratives rests within you.

CONFIDENCE-BUILDING EXERCISES FOR EVERYDAY LEADERSHIP

Integrating confidence-building exercises into your daily routine can make a significant difference in how you perceive yourself and how others perceive you. These practices are not just about quick fixes or temporary boosts, they are about creating habits that reinforce your belief in your abilities. One such exercise is power posing, a technique researched and popularized for its ability to influence our mental state. By adopting expansive postures, you signal confidence to your brain, which helps reduce stress and increase feelings of empowerment. Imagine standing tall, feet apart, arms on hips, just before a big presentation. This simple pose can alter your mindset, preparing you to face challenges with assurance.

Daily journaling is another powerful tool. It offers a space to reflect on experiences, emotions, and insights. Begin each day with a prompt focused on self-reflection, such as "What is one thing I can do today that aligns with my values?" or "What did I learn from yesterday's challenges?" This practice encourages introspection and helps clarify your thoughts, making you more aware of your strengths and areas for growth. Over time, these reflections build a roadmap of personal development, reinforcing your confidence by highlighting progress and learning.

Goals are the stepping stones to greater achievements, yet they often feel daunting. Start small. Set achievable goals that push you slightly out of your comfort zone but remain within reach. For instance, if public speaking raises anxiety, aim to contribute one point in a meeting. Once achieved, this success becomes a building block for larger goals. Using goal-setting templates can help structure your ambitions, breaking them into manageable tasks. Each completed task boosts self-esteem and propels you toward your larger objectives.

Celebrating small wins is crucial in maintaining motivation and reinforcing confidence. It's easy to overlook minor achievements in the hustle of daily life, but acknowledging them fuels continued progress. Whether it's completing a challenging project or simply tackling a difficult conversation, take a moment to recognize these victories. Consider maintaining a list of these wins in a visible place where you can revisit them during moments of doubt. This practice not only reinforces your capabilities but also cultivates gratitude for the journey itself.

Creating a confidence journal is an effective way to document your growth and reflections. Dedicate a notebook to capturing daily affirmations, personal victories, and reflections on challenges overcome. Include templates for tracking progress over time, noting patterns in your confidence levels, and identifying triggers for doubt. This journal becomes a tangible record of your evolution, offering insights during times when self-belief wavers. Revisiting past entries can serve as a reminder of how far you've come and the resilience you've developed.

Confidence Journal Template

Date:

Daily Affirmation:

Today's Goal:

Achievements:

Reflections: What did I learn today? How did I overcome challenges?

Gratitude: What am I grateful for today?

By consistently engaging with these exercises, you create a cycle of positive reinforcement that strengthens your leadership capabilities daily. Incorporating these practices into your life doesn't require drastic changes but rather small, conscious efforts that accumulate over time. Each exercise contributes to a foundation of confidence that supports you through both triumphs and trials.

This isn't about transforming into someone you're not, it's about uncovering the confident leader you already are. With each practice, you reinforce the truth that your voice matters and your contributions are valuable. These habits help cultivate an inner resilience that stands strong against external pressures and societal expectations. As you navigate your leadership path, these exercises serve as reliable tools, helping to maintain focus on what truly matters: leading authentically and confidently in all aspects of life.

BUILDING A SUPPORTIVE INNER DIALOGUE

The conversations we have in our heads often shape our realities more than the words spoken around us. This inner dialogue is a powerful force, a reflection of our deepest beliefs about ourselves and our capabilities. It can be a source of strength or a drain on our confidence, depending on whether it's positive or negative. Positive inner dialogue encourages, uplifts, and reassures us, serving as a silent cheerleader rooting for our success. Negative dialogue, on the other hand, often echoes doubts and fears, questioning our worth and potential. Recognizing the distinction between these two types of dialogues is the first step toward cultivating an empowering mindset.

To transform negative self-talk into positive affirmations, we must first identify the patterns of thought that undermine our confidence. Reframing is a technique that allows us to shift perspective, to view challenges not as insurmountable obstacles but as opportunities for growth. For instance, when faced with a daunting task, instead of thinking, "I can't do this," try reframing it as, "This is challenging, but I am capable of finding a solution." This subtle shift in language can have profound effects on how we perceive our abilities. Positive affirmations tailored to leadership scenarios further reinforce this shift. Phrases like "I am a competent leader" or "My voice matters in this meeting" can become mantras that bolster self-assurance.

Emotional intelligence plays a crucial role in shaping our inner dialogue. It enhances self-awareness and helps us regulate emotions that can cloud judgment or fuel self-doubt. By understanding and managing our emotions, we gain control over our internal narrative, ensuring it reflects our true capabilities rather than fleeting insecurities. Empathy mapping, typically used to understand others' perspectives, can be applied to self-understanding. By mapping out our emotions and responses, we gain insights into what triggers negative thoughts and how we can counteract them with empathy toward ourselves.

To ensure long-term improvement in inner dialogue, it's essential to integrate practices that support sustained growth. Weekly reflection exercises offer an opportunity to assess progress and recalibrate goals. These reflections should focus on acknowledging achievements, identifying areas for improvement, and setting intentions for the coming week. By doing so, you create a feedback loop that encourages continuous development. Additionally, exploring literature on emotional intelligence can provide a deeper understanding of how emotions influence thoughts and behaviors. Books such as "Emotional Intelligence Decoded", by Freedom Publications, offer insights and strategies for enhancing emotional intelligence and refining inner dialogue.

Weekly Reflection Exercise

1. **Achievements:** What did I accomplish this week that I am proud of?
2. **Challenges:** What obstacles did I face, and how did I overcome them?
3. **Emotions:** How did I feel throughout the week? What triggered those emotions?
4. **Intentions:** What are my goals for next week? How can I maintain a positive mindset?

By actively engaging with these exercises and resources, you maintain a supportive inner dialogue that not only boosts confidence but also prepares you to handle future challenges with grace and resilience. This ongoing commitment to nurturing your inner voice ensures that it remains a source of strength rather than doubt.

In embracing these practices, remember that change takes time and patience. It's not about silencing every doubt but about amplifying the voice that believes in your potential. As you navigate your path in leadership and life, let your inner dialogue be your ally, a constant reminder of your worth and capability. With each positive affirmation and reframed thought, you build a foundation of self-trust that empowers you to lead with authenticity and purpose. This inner work is as vital as any skill or strategy in your leadership toolkit, for it shapes how you perceive yourself and interact with the world around you.

As you continue to cultivate this supportive inner dialogue, know that it's an ongoing process of growth and reflection, a journey toward becoming the confident leader you aspire to be.

2

MASTERING ASSERTIVE COMMUNICATION

BREAKING DOWN BARRIERS TO ASSERTIVE COMMUNICATION

I magine sitting in a meeting, brimming with ideas, yet finding yourself unable to express them. This scenario is all too familiar for many women, often rooted in deep-seated barriers to assertive communication. These barriers aren't just personal hurdles; they're intricately woven into societal fabric, influenced by social conditioning and gender roles that have long dictated how women should speak and behave. From a young age, many of us are taught to be polite, accommodating, and agreeable, traits that often suppress assertiveness. This internalized expectation to maintain harmony can lead to a fear of conflict or confrontation, leaving us hesitant to voice differing opinions or challenge the status quo.

The fear of conflict is another formidable barrier. For many, the idea of confrontation is synonymous with discomfort and anxiety. This fear can stem from past experiences where expressing oneself led to negative outcomes, or from a generalized belief that conflict should be avoided at all costs. However, avoiding conflict often means sacrificing our own needs and opinions, leading to frustration and resentment.

To overcome these barriers, we must first acknowledge them. Recognizing these psychological and social influences is the first step toward dismantling their power. Active listening exercises can be a transformative tool in this process. By truly focusing on what others are saying, we can respond more thoughtfully and assertively. This practice not only enhances our communication skills but also builds trust and respect in professional relationships.

Role-playing scenarios can also be incredibly beneficial. By simulating challenging interactions in a safe environment, we can experiment with different responses and receive feedback on our approach. This rehearsal builds confidence, making real-life situations less daunting. Consider pairing up with a trusted friend or colleague to practice these scenarios, focusing on maintaining a calm demeanor and clear articulation of your points.

Setting boundaries is another crucial aspect of assertive communication. Clear boundaries help define what is acceptable in both personal and professional interactions, ensuring mutual respect and understanding. When we articulate our limits, we communicate self-respect and demand the same from others. It's essential to remember that setting boundaries is not selfish, it's a necessary component of healthy communication.

To aid in boundary-setting, templates can be valuable tools. A boundary-setting template might include phrases like, "I am uncomfortable when..." or "I need time to consider this before making a decision." These structures provide a framework for expressing boundaries clearly and respectfully.

Interactive Element: Boundary-Setting Exercise

Take a moment to reflect on areas where you feel your boundaries are often crossed. Write down specific scenarios, such as being expected to work late without notice or being interrupted during meetings. Use the template provided to draft boundary statements for each scenario. Practice these statements aloud until they feel natural and confident.

Real-life examples can illustrate the power of effective boundary enforcement. Consider a colleague who consistently interrupts you during meetings. By setting a boundary, such as saying, "I would like to finish my point before we move on", you assert your right to be heard without escalating tension. Over time, these boundaries become second nature, paving the way for more assertive communication.

Self-confidence plays an integral role in our ability to communicate assertively. When we believe in our own worth and capabilities, we're more likely to express ourselves openly and without fear. Confidence-building exercises tailored specifically for communication can enhance this skill. These might include practicing assertive body language, maintaining eye contact, or using a firm yet approachable tone.

Engaging in regular self-reflection can also bolster confidence. Take time each day to acknowledge your achievements and strengths, no matter how small they may seem. This practice reinforces a positive self-image and reminds you of your value as a communicator.

In mastering assertive communication, remember that it's not about changing who you are but about embracing your voice with confidence and clarity. Each step you take towards breaking down these barriers brings you closer to leading with authenticity and purpose.

TECHNIQUES FOR BEING HEARD WITHOUT BEING PERCEIVED NEGATIVELY

Navigating communication in professional environments often feels like a delicate dance, particularly for us women. The challenge lies in expressing your thoughts assertively without being labeled as aggressive or pushy. Gender dynamics can play a significant role in how communication is perceived. Studies show that men and women often face different expectations when it comes to their communication styles. Women are sometimes expected to be more accommodating, which can lead to their assertiveness being misinterpreted as abrasiveness. Understanding these gendered communication patterns is crucial. By recognizing these biases, you can strategically navigate conversations to ensure your voice is heard. Consider case studies of women who have successfully managed these dynamics. Their strategies can serve as valuable lessons, offering practical insights into how subtle shifts in communication can alter perceptions.

The key to clear and respectful communication lies in how you frame your thoughts. Techniques like using "I-statements" allow you to express your feelings and needs without sounding accusatory. Instead of saying, "You never listen to me," try saying, "I feel unheard when I'm interrupted." This approach focuses on your experience rather than placing blame, fostering a more constructive dialogue. Maintaining a neutral tone also helps in reducing defensiveness from others. Practice speaking in a calm, steady voice, even when discussing contentious issues. This neutrality communicates respect and professionalism, encouraging others to engage with your message rather than your delivery.

Non-verbal communication is another powerful tool in your arsenal. Your body language and facial expressions can either reinforce or undermine your words. Assertive body language includes standing or sitting up straight, which conveys confidence and readiness. Ensure your gestures are open rather than closed or defensive, like crossing your arms, which might suggest discomfort or resistance. Eye contact is equally important, it shows engagement and sincerity. Practice maintaining eye contact to foster connection and trust during interactions. Simple exercises, like practicing conversations in front of a mirror, can help refine these non-verbal cues.

Receiving feedback positively is as important as delivering your message assertively. Feedback is an opportunity for growth, but it can sometimes feel personal or critical. Developing active feedback loops involves listening to the feedback without interrupting or immediately defending your actions. Allow the person to express their observations fully before responding. Once you've received the feedback, thank the person for their insights. This demonstrates openness and respect for their perspective. Constructive criticism acceptance is about separating the message from the messenger. Focus on the content of the feedback rather than who is delivering it, and consider how the feedback aligns with your personal and professional goals.

Case Study: Navigating Gendered Communication Patterns

Consider Maria, a manager in a tech company where male voices typically dominate meetings. Maria noticed her suggestions were often overlooked until reiterated by a male colleague. Frustrated, she decided to change her approach. She began using "I-statements" to articulate her ideas and ensured her body language projected confidence by maintaining eye contact and using open gestures. Maria also practiced receiving feedback graciously, viewing it as a tool for refinement rather than criticism. Over time, her assertiveness was recognized positively, and her contributions gained the respect they deserved.

Incorporating these techniques into your communication style takes practice, but the benefits are worth the effort. As you refine your approach, you'll find that not only does your message come across more clearly, but it also commands respect and attention without negative connotations. This transformation won't happen overnight, it's a gradual process of adjustment and self-awareness. The goal is to communicate with impact, ensuring your ideas are heard and valued in any setting you find yourself in.

Your assertiveness isn't just about speaking louder, but about ensuring your voice resonates with authenticity and confidence. These strategies empower you to navigate complex communication landscapes with ease, allowing you to maintain your dignity and assertiveness without compromise.

DEVELOPING YOUR EXECUTIVE PRESENCE

Executive presence is a term that gets tossed around a lot, but what does it truly mean? At its core, executive presence is about how you project confidence, competence, and credibility in every interaction. It's the way you carry yourself that commands respect and inspires others to follow your lead. The components of executive presence are multifaceted. Gravitas is the quiet strength that underlies your actions, fostering trust and authority. Communication is your ability to articulate ideas clearly and persuasively, ensuring your voice resonates. And then, there's appearance, not about fitting a mold, but about presenting yourself in a way that reflects your professionalism and respect for the role you play.

Authenticity plays a pivotal role in cultivating executive presence. When you're genuine, people sense it. Authenticity fosters trust and builds connections that are vital for effective leadership. Think about the last time you connected with someone who was unapologetically themselves. Their authenticity made you feel at ease, didn't it? Exercises in self-presentation can help you harness this power. Start by reflecting on what makes you unique, your values, strengths, and experiences. Incorporate these elements into your leadership style, allowing your true self to shine through every interaction.

Enhancing executive presence involves practical techniques that can be integrated into your daily routine. Voice modulation exercises are an excellent starting point. Your voice is a powerful tool; how you use it can drastically change perceptions. Practice varying your pitch, pace, and volume to convey confidence and keep listeners engaged. Additionally, consider the impact of your appearance. Dressing appropriately for your environment shows respect for those around you and boosts your self-esteem. While there's no one-size-fits-all approach, aim for attire that aligns with your personal style while maintaining professionalism.

Feedback is invaluable for continuous improvement in executive presence. Peer review sessions offer insights from those who experience your leadership firsthand. Invite colleagues to provide candid feedback on how you come across in meetings or presentations. This feedback helps identify areas for growth that might not be apparent to you. Self-assessment tools are equally useful for tracking progress. Regularly evaluate how well you're embodying the qualities of executive presence and adjust your approach accordingly.

Visual Element: Executive Presence Self-Assessment Tool

Create a chart to rate yourself on key aspects of executive presence: gravitas, communication, appearance, and authenticity. Use a scale from 1 to 5 for each category. Note specific examples where you excelled, or areas needing improvement. Review this chart monthly to monitor progress.

As you refine your executive presence, remember that this isn't about becoming someone you're not. It's about amplifying the best parts of yourself and aligning them with your leadership goals. The authenticity you bring to the table will naturally enhance your presence, making you more relatable and inspiring to others.

Incorporating these strategies into your routine takes time, but the transformation is worth it. You'll notice how much more effectively you can influence and engage those around you. The confidence you project will resonate, making interactions smoother and more impactful. This shift won't happen overnight, but with dedication and practice, you'll cultivate an executive presence that stands out for all the right reasons.

As you continue developing these skills, keep in mind that executive presence isn't just about how others perceive you; it's also about how you perceive yourself. Confidence grows from within, bolstered by a strong sense of self-awareness and a commitment to personal growth. Embrace this aspect of leadership as an ongoing journey—not a destination—and celebrate each step forward as progress toward becoming the leader you're meant to be.

Every interaction offers an opportunity to practice and refine your executive presence further. Engage with intention, listen actively, and respond thoughtfully. Each day provides a chance to hone these skills and build upon the foundation you've established. The more you practice, the more natural it becomes, a seamless extension of who you are as a leader.

With each encounter, you'll find yourself more equipped to handle challenges with poise and navigate complex situations confidently. Your presence will speak volumes before you even say a word, an embodiment of leadership that inspires trust and motivates those around you to achieve their best.

NAVIGATING DIFFICULT CONVERSATIONS WITH CONFIDENCE

Difficult conversations are an inevitable part of professional life. Whether it's addressing performance issues during a review or negotiating a new contract, these discussions require finesse and confidence. Performance reviews, for instance, often bring about anxiety for both parties involved. As a leader, you might worry about how your feedback will be received. On the other hand, when negotiating terms or conditions, the stakes can feel high, with each side striving to reach a beneficial agreement without causing friction. These scenarios demand not only clear communication but also a strong sense of empathy and understanding.

To navigate these challenging interactions effectively, structured approaches can be invaluable. The *DESC model—Describe, Express, Specify, Consequences*—provides a framework that can guide you through the conversation. Start by describing the situation objectively, without attaching blame or emotion. Next, express how the situation impacts you or the team, focusing on feelings and observations. Specify what you need from the other person to resolve the issue, and finally, outline the consequences or benefits of taking the suggested action. This model encourages clarity and openness, fostering a productive dialogue.

Similarly, the *SBI model—Situation, Behavior, Impact—*offers another approach. Begin by describing the specific situation that requires discussion. Identify the behavior observed and its impact on the team or project. This model is particularly effective in performance reviews, where clear examples can help illustrate points constructively. By focusing on behaviors rather than personal attributes, you create a space for growth and improvement.

Managing emotions during these conversations is crucial. Emotions can run high, making it easy to lose composure or say something unintended. Techniques for emotional regulation can help maintain calmness and clarity. Before entering a difficult conversation, take a moment to breathe deeply and ground yourself. Breathing exercises reduce stress levels, allowing you to approach the discussion with a clear mind. Count to four as you inhale deeply through your nose, hold for four counts, and exhale slowly through your mouth for another four. Repeat this cycle until you feel centered and ready.

It's also helpful to prepare mentally by visualizing a positive outcome. Picture the conversation going smoothly, with both parties actively listening and engaging constructively. This mental rehearsal sets a positive tone and helps reduce anxiety.

Approaching difficult conversations with a problem-solving mindset can transform potential conflicts into opportunities for growth. Instead of viewing these discussions as confrontations, see them as chances to collaborate and find solutions. Collaborative problem-solving exercises can foster this mindset. For example, practice brainstorming sessions where all parties contribute ideas freely without judgment. Encourage open dialogue and creativity, focusing on finding common ground and mutually beneficial outcomes.

Reframing conflicts as opportunities is another powerful technique. When disagreements arise, instead of viewing them as obstacles, consider them as catalysts for innovation and change. This perspective shift encourages openness and adaptability, allowing you to approach challenges with curiosity rather than resistance.

As we wrap up this chapter on communication, remember that effective dialogue is not just about speaking but about listening, understanding, and engaging with empathy. Assertive communication is your tool for navigating complex conversations and building stronger relationships both professionally and personally.

In our next chapter, we will explore the art of decision-making and delegation, key skills that complement your communication prowess by enabling you to lead with confidence and clarity.

3

LEVERAGING MENTORSHIP AND NETWORKING

IDENTIFYING AND APPROACHING THE RIGHT MENTOR

In the summer of my first big role, I found myself at a crossroads. I was caught between the excitement of new responsibilities and the daunting task of navigating uncharted territory. That's when I realized I needed guidance beyond textbooks and workshops, a mentor. A mentor is more than just an advisor; they're a beacon of experience and wisdom, illuminating paths you might not see on your own. They offer long-term career guidance, skill development, and personal growth insights that are invaluable as you carve your leadership path.

Finding the right mentor involves more than identifying someone successful. You want a mentor whose industry expertise and experience align with your goals. They should understand the nuances of your field, providing relevant advice that resonates with your professional journey. Equally important is their alignment with your personal values. A mentor should embody principles you admire, serving as a role model in both their professional and personal life. This alignment ensures that their guidance is not only practical but also inspires you to uphold your own standards.

Approaching a potential mentor can feel intimidating, but with the right strategies, it becomes a rewarding endeavor. Start by crafting a compelling introductory email that succinctly outlines your goals and why you've chosen them specifically. This email should reflect genuine admiration for their work and a clear understanding of how their insights could benefit your journey. For instance, mention specific achievements of theirs that resonate with your aspirations or challenge you to grow.

Networking events present another opportunity to connect with potential mentors. Approach these gatherings with a mindset of curiosity and learning. Initiate conversations with genuine questions about their experiences and insights in the industry. Engaging authentically not only builds rapport but also demonstrates your sincerity in seeking guidance, rather than just ticking off a networking checkbox.

Maintaining a productive mentor relationship requires effort from both sides. Regular check-ins are crucial, they ensure that both you and your mentor stay aligned on goals and progress. Schedule periodic feedback sessions to discuss achievements, challenges, and areas for growth. These sessions foster accountability and provide opportunities for reflection on both ends.

Clear expectations form the foundation of any successful mentorship. At the outset, define what you hope to achieve through this relationship and what your mentor can expect from you in terms of commitment and engagement. This mutual understanding paves the way for a fruitful partnership, where both parties feel valued and respected.

Textual Element: Mentor-Mentee Checklist

- *Initial Contact:* Craft a personalized email or message that clearly states your intentions.
- *Goal Alignment:* Discuss and set clear goals for the mentorship relationship.
- *Regular Engagement:* Schedule consistent meetings to review progress.
- *Feedback Loop:* Establish an open channel for ongoing feedback.
- *Respect Boundaries:* Acknowledge professional and personal boundaries to maintain a healthy relationship dynamic.

This checklist serves as a guide to nurturing a mentorship that is not only productive but also enriching for both you and your mentor. The journey with a mentor is one marked by growth, challenge, and transformation. It's about discovering new perspectives, gaining confidence in your abilities, and building a network that supports your ambitions.

Mentorship is more than just absorbing knowledge, it's about fostering connections that propel you forward. As you engage with these strategies, remember that every interaction is an opportunity to learn, grow, and inspire others along the way.

BUILDING YOUR NETWORKING NINJA SKILLS

Networking isn't just about swapping business cards or LinkedIn connections. It's a dynamic process that can open doors to opportunities you might not even know existed. Imagine having access to the latest industry trends, insights that keep you at the cutting edge. Networking can provide that edge, offering opportunities for collaboration and partnerships that drive your projects forward. It's about building a web of connections that supports and elevates you, providing the insights and opportunities that propel your career or business to new heights.

To build an effective network, start with a compelling elevator pitch. This isn't just a quick introduction, it's your chance to make a memorable impression. Your pitch should communicate who you are, what you do, and what you're passionate about, all in the time it takes to ride an elevator. Practice until it feels natural. This concise introduction can be the key to unlocking deeper conversations and connections.

Active listening is another crucial skill. It's about more than hearing words; it's about understanding underlying messages and emotions. Ask engaging questions that show genuine interest in others' experiences and perspectives. This approach not only enriches your understanding but also makes others feel valued and respected, laying the groundwork for meaningful relationships.

In today's digital age, online platforms are invaluable for expanding your networking reach. Begin with LinkedIn, optimizing your profile to showcase your skills and achievements. A polished profile acts as your digital business card, inviting others to connect with you professionally. Engage with content relevant to your field, share articles, and participate in discussions. This active presence positions you as a thought leader and keeps you visible to potential connections.

Join industry forums and groups online where professionals gather to exchange ideas. Participate in these discussions, offering insights and learning from others. These virtual spaces can be as influential as in-person meetings, allowing you to connect with individuals globally who share your interests and goals.

Networking settings vary widely, from formal conferences to casual meet-and-greets. At conferences and seminars, approach networking with a plan. Identify key speakers or attendees you wish to connect with and prepare thoughtful questions or comments. This preparation shows your interest and thoughtfulness, making interactions more impactful.

Virtual networking events require a slightly different approach. In these settings, ensure your technology is set up for success, clear audio, good lighting, and a distraction-free environment help make a positive impression. Engage actively in breakout sessions or chats, where you can share insights or ask questions in smaller groups.

Remember, networking isn't just about taking; it's about giving too. Share your knowledge and resources freely, helping others as you build connections. This reciprocity strengthens relationships and establishes you as a generous and valuable network member.

These strategies transform networking from a chore into an enriching practice that continuously enriches your professional life. Each interaction is a chance to learn something new or to discover an unexpected opportunity. Networking isn't limited by geography or industry; it's a universal tool for growth and connection. As you refine these skills, you'll find yourself becoming not just a participant in your industry but an active contributor and influencer.

The more you engage with these techniques, the more natural they become. Soon, you'll find yourself effortlessly weaving networking into everyday interactions, whether online or offline. It becomes second nature, a part of how you operate both professionally and personally. You'll discover that networking is less about collecting contacts and more about cultivating relationships that matter.

Your network becomes a living ecosystem, rich with diversity and potential, constantly evolving as you grow and change. This ecosystem supports you through career transitions, entrepreneurial ventures, or any path you choose to follow. It's a reminder that while individual effort is crucial, the power of connection amplifies our capabilities beyond measure.

So embrace the potential of networking with open arms and an open mind. Each interaction holds the promise of learning something new or contributing something valuable. Your network is your foundation; nurture it well, and it will support you in ways you might never have expected.

Networking isn't just a skill, it's an invitation to be part of something larger than yourself, a community of like-minded individuals striving toward shared goals. As you develop your skills, remember that the impact of every conversation can ripple far beyond its initial exchange.

CREATING A CIRCLE OF INFLUENCE

Imagine your circle of influence as a dynamic force field that shapes and elevates your leadership journey. This circle isn't just about who's in your contact list, it's about the people who actively contribute to your decision-making and growth. These are the individuals who challenge your thinking, open up opportunities, and support your endeavors. Think of it as a personal board of directors, where each member offers unique insights and strengths. They help you see beyond the immediate, encouraging you to take calculated risks and explore new possibilities. A robust circle of influence not only provides personal growth but also broadens your professional horizons, offering a support system that is both nurturing and motivating.

Identifying key individuals for this circle requires a strategic approach. Start by looking at industry leaders whose work you admire. These are the pioneers whose paths you want to emulate or learn from. Their expertise can offer guidance on navigating the complexities of your industry. Additionally, engage with peers and colleagues who share similar aspirations. These are your allies in the trenches, facing similar challenges and celebrating victories alongside you. Together, you can share resources and insights that propel each other forward. Don't overlook those just outside your immediate professional sphere; diversity in perspective can provide unexpected insights that enrich your growth.

Once you've identified potential circle members, focus on strengthening these connections. Regular communication is key. This doesn't mean constant contact but rather meaningful updates and interactions that keep the relationship vibrant. Share your achievements and challenges openly, inviting feedback and advice. This transparency fosters trust and makes them invested in your success. Collaborative projects are another excellent way to deepen these ties. Working together on initiatives not only leverages each person's strengths but also solidifies your bond through shared goals and outcomes. These experiences create a sense of camaraderie and mutual respect, essential elements in any influential network.

Reciprocity forms the backbone of any effective circle of influence. It's about giving as much as receiving, ensuring that the relationship remains balanced and beneficial for all parties involved. Offer help to those within your circle whenever possible, whether through sharing knowledge, providing introductions, or lending a hand during challenging times. Your willingness to support others strengthens the bonds within the circle and demonstrates your commitment to collective success. Additionally, share valuable resources and information that might benefit others. Whether it's an article, a new tool, or an upcoming event, these small gestures show that you're actively contributing to their growth.

Interactive Element: Building Your Circle of Influence

Create a list of individuals you believe could form your circle of influence. Categorize them based on their roles; mentors, peers, industry leaders and note what each brings to the table. Next to each name, write down one action you can take to strengthen that connection, whether it's scheduling a coffee meeting, sending an article of interest, or initiating a collaborative project.

This exercise is not just about plotting names on paper, it's about visualizing the ecosystem of support around you and taking concrete steps to nurture it. Your circle of influence is a living entity that evolves as you grow in your career and life. It's a testament to the power of connection and collaboration, proving that while individual effort is essential, the strength of a community can be transformative. As you cultivate this circle, remember that every interaction is an opportunity to learn and contribute positively. Building such a network takes time and intentional effort, but the rewards are immeasurable.

Your circle influences not only what you achieve but also how you perceive and tackle challenges. These connections can offer perspective during tough decisions or encouragement when you're on the brink of something new. They help anchor you in reality while encouraging you to stretch beyond your comfort zone. This synergy is what makes your circle of influence so powerful, it's where shared dreams meet shared actions, creating ripples that extend far beyond individual aspirations.

In nurturing this circle, you're not just enhancing your leadership potential; you're also contributing to a broader community of empowered individuals who support and uplift one another. The relationships you build today lay the groundwork for not only personal success but also for a legacy of collaboration and mutual growth that benefits everyone involved.

LEVERAGING PROFESSIONAL NETWORKS FOR CAREER ADVANCEMENT

Building a robust professional network is like constructing a bridge to future opportunities. It's not just about who you know but how you engage with them. Strong networks can propel your career by providing access to job openings and promotions that might otherwise remain hidden. These connections often offer a backstage pass to roles not advertised to the public. Mentorship and sponsorship within your network can also play pivotal roles in career advancement. A mentor might guide you through career decisions, while a sponsor actively advocates for your progression and visibility within the organization, creating pathways that align with your aspirations.

To maximize the potential of your network, it's important to be proactive. Start by seeking referrals and recommendations from trusted contacts. A well-placed recommendation can open doors that even your resume may not. When you receive such opportunities, act on them swiftly and decisively, showcasing your readiness and enthusiasm. Engaging in knowledge-sharing sessions is another effective strategy. Organize or participate in these sessions to exchange insights and experiences. They're not just about absorbing information; they're about contributing your unique perspective, which can elevate your standing within your network.

Networks are also invaluable for skill development. Learning doesn't only happen in classrooms or formal settings; it can occur through workshops and training sessions organized by your network. These events are often tailored to industry trends and emerging technologies, keeping you at the forefront of your field. By actively participating, you sharpen your skills and demonstrate a commitment to growth. This involvement shows others that you're an asset worth investing in, further cementing your place within the network.

Continuous expansion of your network is crucial. Stagnation is the enemy of growth, so remain open to new connections. Joining industry groups and associations introduces you to fresh perspectives and ideas, broadening your understanding of the field. These groups often host events and discussions that challenge you to think differently and innovate. Additionally, look beyond your immediate industry for potential connections. Building relationships outside your usual circles can provide insights into different markets or sectors, enriching your overall professional experience.

Networking isn't just about personal gain; it's about mutual benefit. When you focus on adding value to others' journeys, you naturally enhance your own. This reciprocity fosters a supportive environment where everyone thrives. As you connect with others, remember that every interaction is an opportunity to learn and grow together.

Resource List: Expanding Your Professional Network

- **Industry Associations:** Organizations that offer networking events, seminars, and resources specific to your field.
- **Online Platforms:** Websites like *LinkedIn* where you can connect with professionals globally.

- **Workshops/Training Sessions:** Events where you can develop skills while meeting new people.
- **Mentorship Programs:** Initiatives that pair you with experienced professionals for guidance.

In wrapping up this chapter, remember that networking is an ongoing process, not a one-time task. It's about cultivating relationships that last, adapting to changes, and embracing new opportunities as they arise. Your network is not just a collection of contacts, it's a living ecosystem that supports your professional journey at every stage. As we move forward, our next chapter will explore decision-making and delegation, crucial skills that complement networking by enabling you to act on the opportunities your network provides.

4

NAVIGATING GENDER BIAS AND WORKPLACE CHALLENGES

UNDERSTANDING AND COMBATING GENDER BIAS

Imagine being in a meeting, presenting an idea you've meticulously crafted, only to find it dismissed or attributed to someone else. It's a scene that resonates with many women, a subtle yet profound manifestation of gender bias. This bias isn't always blatant, more often, it lurks in the shadows of professional interactions, affecting how women's contributions are perceived and valued. Gender bias refers to prejudices or discrimination based on gender, impacting opportunities and career progression. It can manifest as overt actions, like explicit pay disparities, or more covert forms, such as microaggressions or being perpetually interrupted in discussions. These biases, sometimes deeply ingrained in workplace cultures, can create barriers that make it harder for women to ascend the corporate ladder.

The prevalence of gender bias varies across industries, but its impact is pervasive. For instance, studies reveal that women are underrepresented in leadership roles, despite making up a significant portion of the workforce. A significant report highlights that while women's representation in C-suite positions has increased from 17% to 29% since 2015, progress remains slow at managerial levels (McKinsey & Company, 2024). The disparity in pay is another critical issue. Women often earn less than their male counterparts for similar work, a reality that undermines equity in professional settings. These patterns not only stall individual careers but also stifle organizational growth by limiting diverse perspectives at decision-making tables.

Common scenarios where gender bias surfaces include unequal pay for similar roles and disproportionate representation in leadership positions. Unequal pay remains a persistent issue despite various initiatives aimed at closing the gap. Women are often paid less than men for equivalent roles, a disparity that adds up over time and affects long-term financial stability. Similarly, leadership roles are skewed towards men, with fewer women occupying top executive positions. This lack of representation can perpetuate a cycle where male-dominated perspectives shape organizational policies and cultures, further sidelining women's voices.

To combat these biases, strategic action is essential. One effective approach is developing an allyship with male colleagues. Allies can play a pivotal role in advocating for gender equality by challenging biased behaviors and supporting women's advancement. Engaging in bias training workshops is another proactive measure. These sessions increase awareness of unconscious biases and equip participants with tools to counteract them. Moreover, advocating for policy changes within organizations can lead to systemic improvements. This includes pushing for transparent pay structures and equitable hiring practices that prioritize diversity.

Organizational culture plays a crucial role in either perpetuating or dismantling gender bias. Fostering an inclusive culture requires deliberate effort and commitment from leadership. Creating diversity and inclusion committees can be a starting point. These groups focus on implementing strategies that promote equal opportunities and address biases. Establishing mentorship programs for underrepresented groups is equally important. Such programs provide guidance and support, helping women navigate challenges and develop leadership skills.

Interactive Element: Reflection Exercise

Reflect on your experiences with gender bias in the workplace. Consider moments when you felt sidelined or undervalued. Write down these instances and identify patterns or triggers that may have contributed to them. Next, brainstorm actionable steps you can take to address these challenges, whether it's discussing your concerns with HR or seeking mentorship from an ally.

This exercise isn't just about acknowledgment; it's about empowerment. By understanding the nuances of gender bias and actively seeking solutions, you take control of your professional narrative. The path to equality requires collective action and individual resilience, each step building towards a more inclusive future where talent and potential are recognized regardless of gender.

STRATEGIES FOR GAINING VISIBILITY AND RECOGNITION

In the fast-paced professional world, visibility isn't just about being seen. It's about being recognized and valued for your contributions. This recognition is crucial because, without it, even your most remarkable and groundbreaking achievements can inadvertently fall by the wayside, limiting your potential for growth and advancement. Consider visibility as your personal professional spotlight, an indispensable tool that illuminates your unique skills and ensures you remain memorable when opportunities arise or when critical decisions are made. Being at the forefront of high-profile projects and initiatives can significantly enhance your visibility. It is not just the act of participating but rather positioning yourself in roles that demand leadership, creativity, and innovation that positions you as an indispensable asset to your team. Recognition through awards or accolades further cements your reputation, serving as tangible proof of your capabilities and dedication that others can see and appreciate. These recognitions aren't merely decorative ornaments; they are powerful endorsements that can propel you to new heights within your career, opening doors that were previously closed.

To enhance your professional visibility, consider volunteering for cross-departmental teams or projects. This approach not only broadens your professional network but also showcases your versatility and adaptability across different functions and settings. Engaging actively with various departments allows you to display some of your most valuable skills, such as adaptability and adept problem-solving, crucial traits for those aspiring to leadership roles or positions of higher responsibility. Presenting at esteemed industry conferences is yet another effective strategy that benefits multifold. It positions you as a thought leader and expert in your field. When you share your insights, findings, or innovative ideas with your peers, you are not only highlighting your knowledge but also your dedication to advancing industry standards, contributing to the broader body of knowledge. This exposure can lead to invaluable new connections, potential collaborations, and even unexpected job offers, all stemming from a single insightful and well-received presentation.

Self-promotion, though often misunderstood as bragging, is an important aspect of gaining recognition. It's not about boasting or being pretentious but rather about effectively communicating your achievements, skills, and contributions. Creating a personal achievement portfolio can be a practical and powerful way to document and display your successes. This portfolio could include detailed project outlines, measurable outcomes, visuals, and testimonials from colleagues, mentors, or clients who can vouch for your work. It serves as a ready reference during performance reviews or interviews, allowing you to articulate your contributions clearly and convincingly. Sharing these successes in team meetings, newsletters, or even informal gatherings keeps your accomplishments on the radar, ensuring they're acknowledged by those who matter most in your professional journey.

Building and nurturing a strong professional reputation goes hand in hand with visibility and recognition, each feeding into the other. Consistently delivering high-quality work should be the foundational pillar of your reputation. When you regularly exceed expectations, you establish yourself as a reliable and competent professional. This level of reliability builds trust with your colleagues and superiors alike, positioning you as a highly regarded team member. Developing expertise in a niche area can further enhance your reputation. Specializing in a particular domain sets you apart, marking you as the go-to person for specific challenges or initiatives. This specialized expertise not only adds depth and dimension to your professional profile but also enhances your leverage in career negotiations.

The journey to gaining visibility and recognition is an ongoing process, one that does not conclude with a single achievement. Each proactive step you take to enhance your presence in the workplace contributes to a larger narrative of growth, resilience, and success. Visibility, recognition, self-promotion, and reputation, each element interlinks intricately with the others, creating a cohesive strategy that empowers you to take control of your career trajectory. While these strategies require a concerted effort and unwavering dedication, they are investments in your future self that can yield substantial returns, paving the way for greater professional satisfaction and personal fulfillment.

OVERCOMING IMPOSTER SYNDROME

Imposter syndrome is that nagging feeling of inadequacy, the voice in your head saying you don't belong here, even when all evidence points otherwise. This psychological phenomenon can be particularly crippling for women striving to make their mark in professional spaces. It creates a cycle of self-doubt that affects every decision, making you question your worth and abilities. This constant questioning can slow career progress, causing you to shy away from opportunities or second-guess your achievements. Over time, the weight of imposter syndrome can erode confidence and hold back even the most talented individuals from reaching their potential.

Recognizing the triggers and symptoms of imposter syndrome is crucial. Perfectionism often fuels this condition, with the relentless pursuit of flawlessness leading to inevitable feelings of failure when perfection isn't achieved. The fear of making mistakes or not meeting unrealistic standards can paralyze you, keeping you from taking necessary risks or exploring new avenues. Another common trigger is the tendency to compare oneself to others. In a world where social media and professional platforms portray curated versions of success, it's easy to feel like everyone else has it together except you. This comparison trap deepens self-doubt, making it seem like you're the only one struggling.

There are ways to combat these feelings and reclaim your confidence. Cognitive restructuring exercises can be powerful tools for changing the narrative in your head. These exercises help you challenge negative thoughts and replace them with positive affirmations and realistic perspectives. For example, when you catch yourself thinking, "I don't deserve this role," counter it with evidence of your accomplishments and the skills that got you there. Seeking feedback and mentorship for validation is another effective strategy. Constructive feedback from trusted peers or mentors can provide an external perspective, reminding you of your strengths and contributions. Mentors, in particular, offer valuable insights, helping you see beyond your doubts and recognize your potential.

Hearing stories from women who've successfully navigated imposter syndrome can offer both inspiration and practical guidance. Take Maya, a marketing director who once felt out of place among her more experienced peers. She often stayed silent in meetings, worried her ideas wouldn't measure up. However, through cognitive restructuring and seeking mentorship, she began to see the value in her unique perspective. Her mentor encouraged her to speak up more often, highlighting her fresh approach as a strength rather than a liability. Over time, Maya's confidence grew, leading to more active participation and recognition from her peers.

Similarly, consider the story of Emma, who initially struggled with imposter syndrome as she transitioned into a leadership role. The pressure of proving herself in a new position was overwhelming. Emma worked closely with a mentor who had faced similar challenges, learning techniques to manage her self-doubt. She practiced shifting her focus from perceived shortcomings to her achievements and strengths. This shift allowed her to embrace her leadership capabilities fully, ultimately earning respect from her team and peers.

These narratives highlight a crucial lesson: overcoming imposter syndrome isn't about eliminating doubt completely, but about managing it effectively. It's about acknowledging those moments of insecurity and choosing not to let them define your path. Each step taken towards conquering imposter syndrome is a step towards embracing your authentic self and recognizing the value you bring to every table.

In navigating through these feelings, remember that you're not alone. Many women experience similar struggles, silently battling the same doubts in their professional lives. Sharing experiences and supporting each other creates a community of resilience and empowerment. It's about lifting each other up and reminding one another that we belong here, not by chance but by merit.

So when imposter syndrome rears its head, face it with courage and determination. Use it as an opportunity to grow and redefine what success means for you personally. Embrace the discomfort as part of the process, knowing that each challenge faced is a testament to your strength and perseverance.

BALANCING PROFESSIONAL AMBITIONS WITH PERSONAL LIFE

The intricate dance of balancing professional aspirations with the necessities of personal life can often feel as precarious as walking a proverbial tightrope suspended high above the ground. You're certainly not navigating this path on your own. This balancing act is a shared reality for innumerable women who find themselves navigating the ever-complex world of today. These women are striving to meet a myriad of societal expectations, reaching for their career goals with both hands while simultaneously fulfilling family obligations and personal responsibilities. Amidst all this, they strive to maintain a semblance of personal fulfillment, which can sometimes seem elusive.

Society, with its ingrained cultural norms, has historically placed a notably heavy burden of expectation on women. The demand is often for them to excel in their careers, achieving professional milestones and earning accolades, all while being the primary nurturers and caretakers at home, ensuring the household runs smoothly. This dual role can, quite understandably, lead to significant time management difficulties. The hours available in one day may seem perpetually insufficient, stretched thin across various commitments. It's no surprise, then, that feelings of being overwhelmed are common, as the pressure to meet these multifaceted demands mounts, creating a scenario where personal self-care or growth is often relegated to the back burner.

Achieving a sustainable work-life balance, one that leads to a harmonious existence, mandates the employment of intentional strategies. One effective approach is to explore flexible work arrangements that fit your lifestyle needs. Many organizations have recognized the importance of such flexibility and now offer telecommuting options, allowing you to work from home. This arrangement provides more control over your schedule, which can be a true game-changer. The reduction in commute times is just the tip of the iceberg, it also allows you to weave your professional duties seamlessly with your personal responsibilities. Another practical technique to enhance productivity is time-blocking. This involves allocating specific, dedicated time slots for various tasks, enabling you to focus with greater intention and preventing your work commitments from spilling into your personal time unabashedly. Such a structured approach allows you to prioritize what genuinely matters, sculpting a more balanced and harmonious rhythm between your work and your life.

Setting clear priorities is fundamental in effectively managing both personal and professional goals. Creating a well-thought-out, values-based priority list can guide you in making decisions and taking actions that align with your core beliefs and long-term objectives. This priority list serves as a compass, steering you through the maze of commitments without losing sight of what is truly important. Equally vital are techniques for saying no to non-essential commitments. While it may not come easy, especially if you're accustomed to being accommodating in various facets of life, learning to say no, politely yet firmly, can liberate time and energy. This newfound space allows for pursuits that deeply resonate with your goals and aspirations, contributing to a more fulfilling life.

Support systems also play an indispensable role in balancing life with work. Tapping into available resources, such as reliable childcare services or solid family support, can significantly relieve some of the pressures associated with managing manifold responsibilities. Additionally, building a network of supportive colleagues can provide both emotional and practical support within your workplace. These connections foster a sense of camaraderie, enabling you to share both challenges and successes with those who truly understand your experiences. Whether it's turning to a trusted friend, mentor, or coworker, having someone to lean on can make the daunting balancing act feel slightly less intimidating.

As we draw this chapter on balancing professional ambitions with personal life to a close, it's important to remember that while these strategies serve as valuable guidance, there is no one-size-fits-all solution to this multifaceted challenge. Each individual's path is unique, intricately shaped by their own circumstances and aspirations. The crucial element lies in discovering what works optimally for you and being adaptable in the face of inevitable change. As we transition into the next chapter, we'll delve into the art of decision-making and delegation, skills paramount to supporting your journey toward effective leadership by empowering you to prioritize and manage responsibilities with enhanced confidence and clarity.

5

CRAFTING YOUR PERSONAL BRAND

DEFINING YOUR PERSONAL BRAND

If you were able to walk into a room and leave an indelible impression without uttering a word, how would you feel? Just as an artist uses colors, brush strokes, and unique styles to create a masterpiece, you can craft a personal brand that is equally distinct and memorable. This brand is the unique blend of your skills, experiences, and values that make you memorable and resonate with others. In today's highly competitive landscape, where everyone is vying for attention, differentiation, the art of standing out, is absolutely pivotal. Your personal brand sets you apart, showcasing what makes you, well, distinctly you. It's not solely about standing out but also about beautifully aligning who you are with what you do, thereby influencing how opportunities present themselves and come your way.

Let's further explore and dive into the essence of personal branding by comparing it to your professional identity or your signature in the career world. It's the way you present yourself to others, highlighting the unique attributes and invaluable contributions you bring to the table. This brand isn't just a corporate buzzword flitting around in cyberspace, it's a strategic tool that can wield influence over career opportunities and how others perceive you. A strong, well-articulated personal brand can open doors to exciting new projects, valuable promotions, and promising partnerships. Essentially, it's about creating a narrative that conveys your strengths and aspirations both clearly and authentically.

To precisely define your personal brand, start by uncovering and identifying your core values and strengths, those unchanging factors that truly represent who you are. These serve as the pillars supporting your brand's sturdy foundation. Core values are those guiding principles that influence your actions and decisions, beautifully reflecting what matters most to you deep down. To uncover these intrinsic values, reflect on past experiences where you felt most fulfilled or proud. What common themes emerge from these moments of triumph and satisfaction? Strengths, on the other hand, are the skills or qualities that come most naturally to you, distinguishing your approach and effectiveness. Utilize assessment tools like *StrengthsFinder* to gain deeper insights and articulate your top talents.

Consistency in branding is crucial for trust-building and reinforcing your identity across different platforms and interactions. Start by developing a personal branding statement, a concise declaration of who you are and what value you bring to the world, along with why it matters. This statement should reflect consistently in both your visual and verbal communications. Whether it's your LinkedIn profile or a succinct elevator pitch, ensuring that your message remains cohesive is key. This harmonized consistency signals professionalism and reliability to those who encounter your brand in various settings.

Articulating your unique value proposition requires clarity and a deep sense of introspection. Think of it as the promise you make to those you engage with, what they can wholeheartedly expect from every interaction with you. Crafting a personal mission statement can aid in this process by defining your purpose and direction, grounded in your overarching goals. Draw inspiration from industry leaders, their compelling value propositions often stem from a profound understanding of their inherent strengths and durable contributions.

Interactive Element: Personal Branding Reflection Exercise

Take a moment to write down three core values and three strengths that define you in your professional journey. Reflect on how these elements have influenced your career choices or interactions in the past, enhancing them or steering them in specific directions. Next, draft a personal branding statement incorporating these aspects, ensuring it is both concise yet impactful, something you'd be proud to share in any professional setting, be it an interview or a networking event.

Your personal brand is not just an exercise in self-promotion; it's a journey of self-actualization deeply rooted in authenticity. It's about stepping into the world as the best version of yourself and allowing others to truly see and appreciate the real you, highlighting your passions, your talents, and your boundless potential. Remember that this brand evolves with you, reflecting your growth, changes, and new directions over time.

As we navigate through this enlightening chapter, continue to relentlessly explore what makes your brand uniquely yours, honing it and nurturing it. Embrace the ongoing journey of self-discovery and expression, knowing that each step and revelation bring you ever closer to leading with unparalleled confidence and clarity in every facet of your life, paving the way for future successes.

INCREASING YOUR VISIBILITY IN THE WORKPLACE

Standing out in the workplace is not just about being seen, it's about being recognized for your contributions and capabilities. This recognition can lead to new opportunities and professional growth that align with your aspirations. One effective way to increase your visibility is by taking the initiative in high-profile projects. Volunteering for tasks that are visible to upper management or that impact the company at large can set you apart as a proactive and committed team member. These projects are often high-stakes and require dedication, but they offer a platform to showcase your skills and leadership potential.

Leading workshops or training sessions is another avenue to enhance your visibility. By sharing your expertise with colleagues, you demonstrate leadership and build your credibility within the organization. These sessions can be tailored to address current challenges or provide new insights that benefit your team. Not only do they highlight your knowledge, but they also position you as a resourceful leader who contributes to the growth and development of others.

In today's digital age, maintaining a strong professional presence online is crucial for personal branding. Optimizing your LinkedIn profile ensures that it reflects your skills, accomplishments, and professional interests. A well-crafted profile attracts attention from recruiters and industry peers, expanding your professional network. Engage with industry content on social media platforms by commenting on articles, sharing insights, or participating in discussions. This active engagement boosts your visibility and establishes you as an informed and involved professional within your field.

Effective self-promotion involves highlighting achievements without coming across as boastful. One approach is to frame accomplishments in terms of team contributions. For instance, instead of saying "I led a successful project," say "Our team delivered exceptional results under my leadership." This approach acknowledges the collective effort while subtly emphasizing your role. Sharing successes in professional forums, whether through company newsletters or industry publications, also helps you gain recognition. These platforms allow you to present your achievements to a broader audience, enhancing visibility beyond your immediate workplace.

Networking plays a pivotal role in increasing workplace visibility. Attending industry conferences and meetups provides opportunities to connect with peers, learn from experts, and discuss emerging trends. These events are not just about collecting business cards; they are about building genuine relationships that can lead to collaborations and career advancements. Networking strategically with key stakeholders within your organization can also enhance your visibility. Building relationships with decision-makers or influencers means they are more likely to consider you for future opportunities or projects.

All these strategies collectively contribute to a well-rounded approach to increasing visibility in the workplace. They require intentional effort and consistency but offer substantial rewards in recognition and career progression. By actively seeking opportunities to showcase your skills and engaging with others both online and offline, you create a professional image that stands out in an increasingly competitive landscape.

But note that this approach is not about creating a false persona, but about amplifying your true strengths and achievements. It's about ensuring that your hard work does not go unnoticed and that you are recognized as a valuable contributor within your organization and industry. As you navigate these strategies, remember that visibility is not just about being seen; it's about being remembered for the right reasons, creating lasting impressions that open doors to new possibilities.

Your visibility in the workplace is a dynamic aspect of your career that evolves as you grow and change. Each interaction, project, or connection adds layers to your professional identity, shaping how others perceive you and what opportunities come your way. The key is to remain authentic, consistent, and proactive in showcasing what makes you unique. In doing so, you not only enhance your career prospects but also inspire others to recognize their potential for growth and impact within their own roles.

PERSONAL BRANDING TECHNIQUES FOR CAREER GROWTH

Your personal brand isn't merely a reflection of your identity; it's a strategic beacon that can significantly drive your career trajectory forward. Imagine it as a carefully sculpted image that not only communicates your strengths and values but also serves as your professional signature in the vast landscape of opportunities. One of the most impactful techniques for capitalizing on this asset is to position yourself as an expert within a niche area. By honing in on a particular specialty, you establish yourself as the go-to individual for targeted challenges and specific issues, thereby enhancing your intrinsic value within your field of operation. This strategic focus not only bolsters your credibility but also paves the way for opportunities that naturally gravitate toward your sphere of expertise. Consider how this specialization might open avenues to innovative projects, collaborations, and roles that align with what you do best. Moreover, aligning your personal brand with your organization's overarching goals and values can propel your career prospects even further. When your brand authentically mirrors the ethos and mission of your workplace, it fosters a harmonious synergy that underscores your position as an essential contributor to collective success. This alignment vividly displays your commitment and adaptability - attributes that hold tremendous value in the eyes of employers.

Moreover, establishing yourself as a thought leader adds significant weight to your career enhancement arsenal. Thought leadership embodies the sharing of novel insights and perspectives that have the power to inspire and influence other professionals within your domain. Delving into this role involves more than just distributing information; it requires engaging others through compelling narratives and actionable ideas. Publishing articles or whitepapers in established industry journals can significantly amplify your voice. Such publications not only demonstrate your comprehensive knowledge but also allow you to partake actively in pivotal industry dialogues, elevating your reputation across the professional landscape. Engaging in speaking opportunities at conferences provides yet another avenue to manifest expertise and build credibility. Whether you are part of an enlightening panel discussion or delivering a keynote speech, sharing your insights with an enthusiastic audience strengthens your standing as a thought leader. These platforms not only bolster your profile but also facilitate numerous networking opportunities, making you a magnet for potential employers or collaborative partners keen to tap into your insights and vision.

Regularly conducting audits of your personal brand is essential to ensure its alignment with your evolving career goals. This continual assessment serves as a roadmap, helping you identify how others perceive your brand in contrast to how you want it to be perceived. By seeking feedback through anonymous surveys or engaging in candid feedback sessions with trusted collaborators, you can garner insightful perspectives vital for your brand evolution. This feedback process reveals whether your personal brand mirrors your intended image and highlights areas ripe for improvement. Employ this information to refine your branding strategies constantly, ensuring they remain supportive of your career aspirations and advancement. These regular audits prevent the risk of stagnation, allowing for necessary adaptability to shifts and maintaining relevance in an increasingly competitive environment.

Adaptability is the cornerstone to sustaining an influential and impactful personal brand. The career environment is perpetually morphing, shaped by rapid technological advancements and fluctuating market demands. Hence, your brand should not be static; it must evolve to reflect these dynamic shifts while remaining anchored in its core values. Consider how professionals in the tech sector continuously update their skill sets and brand narratives to encapsulate emerging trends like artificial intelligence and cybersecurity. This not only keeps their brands relevant but also ensures they remain ahead of the curve. Maintaining relevance can also stem from continual learning and active networking within industry circles. Staying abreast of industry developments is imperative to keeping your brand fresh and alluring.

Integrating these approaches into your personal branding repertoire significantly bolsters career growth by positioning you as an expert, thought leader, and adaptable professional. A well-crafted brand does more than simply define who you are; it strategically harmonizes with your career ambitions, unlocking new opportunities and paving the way for long-term success.

ALIGNING YOUR BRAND WITH YOUR LEADERSHIP STYLE

Imagine your personal brand as the dynamic and sophisticated reflection of your distinctive leadership style, a mirror that not only highlights your strengths but also magnifies and enhances them to a level of excellence. This alignment between your personal brand and leadership style is crucial, functioning as a harmonious symphony where coalescence creates a powerful presence that others naturally recognize and deeply respect. This synthesis is more than just about projecting raw confidence; it's fundamentally about embodying the deeper principles you staunchly stand for and represent. Consider, for instance, leaders whose core brand values are in perfect synchronization with their guiding leadership principles. Such leaders often find their influence extending far beyond their immediate professional spheres because they communicate a coherent and consistent message that resonates with authenticity and integrity across their various audiences.

To delve deeper, imagine a leader renowned for their unwavering transparency and ethical decision-making integrity. If their personal brand eloquently emphasizes these noteworthy traits, it reinforces and fortifies their professional narrative, effectively making their leadership style more compelling and persuasive to diverse audiences. The intersection where brand meets leadership is profoundly pivotal, it's where actual influence is birthed and nurtured. It transcends mere displays of your deeds, immersing into embodying the values that fundamentally underpin your actions and decisions. This harmonious synergy is what fosters enduring trust and credibility, which are invaluable assets in any effective leadership role.

Communicating your leadership style through branding requires deliberate and intentional storytelling. Your unfolding narrative should reflect the remarkable journey you've taken thus far to reach your present position, highlighting pivotal and defining moments that have significantly shaped your overarching leadership philosophy. Whether through engaging interviews, insightful blogs, or thought-provoking social media posts, sharing these stories humanizes your brand, making it relatable, meaningful, and inspiring to diverse audiences. Equally important are visual branding elements that play a vibrant and lively role. Consistent use of specific colors, distinctive logos, and impactful imagery that reflect your leadership qualities can robustly strengthen your brand's identity. A leader celebrated for relentless innovation and creativity might resort to bold colors and modern design elements to vividly convey forward-thinking ideals that serve to inspire.

Building trust and credibility through personal branding involves rigorous consistency, both in grand actions and succinct messaging. When your voiced words align seamlessly with what you actively do, it reinforces your reliability and dependability as a leader. Testimonials and endorsements from credible peers and colleagues can further cement this trust, offering third-party validation of your indispensable capabilities. These endorsements should reflect and align with your leadership qualities, providing tangible and illustrative evidence of your positive impact on others. They serve as robust tools in establishing and reinforcing your credibility within esteemed professional circles.

Authenticity remains the unshakeable cornerstone of aligning brand with leadership style. It involves embracing who you genuinely are and allowing that authenticity to shine fervently through every facet of your brand. Authenticity exercises can help you explore nuanced self-expression, encouraging you to identify and articulate what makes you inherently unique. Avoid falling into the pitfalls of inauthentic branding practices by staying unwaveringly true to your core values and resisting passing trends that don't align with your genuine identity. Authenticity importantly isn't about perfection; it's about being genuine and transparent regarding your strengths and acknowledging the areas poised for growth and development.

As we wrap up this intricate chapter on crafting your personal brand, remember earnestly that alignment with your leadership style is not a one-time task but rather a continuous and evolving practice. Each interaction provides a wonderful opportunity to reinforce your brand's message and eloquently showcase your leadership qualities. This diligent alignment enhances your influence, effectively enabling you to lead with enhanced clarity and impactful foresight. Embrace this dynamic interplay between brand and leadership as a formidable tool for enduring personal and professional growth.

As we seamlessly transition to the next enlightening chapter, we'll delve deeper into decision-making strategies, another critical and quintessential component of effective and insightful leadership. These refined strategies will complement and synergize with the solid foundation you've meticulously built with your personal brand, empowering and equipping you to lead with greater confidence, assuredness, and purpose.

6

ENHANCING EMOTIONAL INTELLIGENCE AND SELF-AWARENESS

UNDERSTANDING THE ROLE OF EMOTIONAL INTELLIGENCE IN LEADERSHIP

Imagine steering a ship through turbulent waters without a compass. That's what leading without emotional intelligence (EI) can feel like. Emotional intelligence is the compass that can guide you through the complexities of leadership. At its core, Emotional Intelligence is about recognizing, understanding, and managing your own emotions while also being sensitive to the emotions of others. This skill set allows you to navigate interpersonal dynamics with grace and effectiveness.

Emotional intelligence consists of several key components: self-awareness, self-regulation, motivation, empathy, and social skills. Self-awareness is your ability to recognize your emotions as they occur, understanding how they affect your thoughts and actions. This awareness forms the foundation for self-regulation, which involves controlling impulsive feelings and behaviors, managing your emotions in healthy ways, and adapting to changing circumstances. Motivation in the context of emotional intelligence is not just about achieving goals but doing so with energy and persistence driven by an intrinsic passion for the work itself. Empathy is the ability to understand others' emotions, allowing you to respond appropriately and build meaningful connections. Finally, social skills involve managing relationships to move people in desired directions, whether you're leading a team or navigating complex negotiations.

The impact of emotional intelligence on leadership effectiveness is profound. Leaders with high emotional intelligence tend to communicate more effectively and collaborate seamlessly within teams. Improved communication stems from the ability to listen actively and articulate thoughts clearly, fostering an environment where ideas flow freely. Enhanced conflict resolution skills are another benefit, as emotional intelligence equips you to address disagreements with tact and empathy, finding common ground without escalating tensions. Leaders who master these aspects create teams that are not only efficient but also harmonious, where each member feels valued and understood.

Moreover, emotional intelligence fosters trust and rapport within teams, strengthening cohesion and building a culture of openness and support. When team members see their leader demonstrating empathy and understanding, they are more likely to mirror these behaviors, creating a positive feedback loop that enhances team dynamics. This environment encourages open dialogue and collaboration, laying the groundwork for innovation and problem-solving. A leader who can empathize with their team members' challenges and aspirations is more likely to inspire loyalty and commitment, driving collective success.

Consider leaders like Jacinda Ardern or Satya Nadella, whose leadership styles exemplify high emotional intelligence. Jacinda Ardern, Prime Minister of New Zealand, is renowned for her empathetic approach to governance. Her response to crises, grounded in compassion and transparency, has earned her global admiration and trust among her constituents. Ardern's ability to connect emotionally with her audience has been pivotal in uniting a diverse nation during challenging times.

Similarly, Satya Nadella, CEO of Microsoft, has transformed the company's culture by prioritizing empathy and collaboration. Under his leadership, Microsoft shifted from a competitive internal culture to one that values openness and learning. Nadella's emphasis on empathy as a core leadership value has fostered an inclusive environment where innovation thrives. His approach demonstrates how emotional intelligence can redefine organizational culture and drive business success.

Textual Element: Reflection on Emotionally Intelligent Leadership

Reflect on a leader you admire for their emotional intelligence, someone whose approach has inspired or influenced you positively. Consider what specific actions or qualities make them stand out. Write down how you can incorporate similar strategies into your own leadership style. This exercise helps you identify practical ways to enhance your emotional intelligence by learning from those who exemplify it.

These examples illustrate that emotional intelligence is not just a soft skill but a strategic advantage in leadership. It empowers you to lead with authenticity and purpose, creating environments where people feel seen and heard. As you cultivate your emotional intelligence, remember that it's an ongoing journey of growth and self-discovery, one that enhances not only your leadership capabilities but also your personal fulfillment and connection to others.

EXERCISES FOR ENHANCING SELF-AWARENESS

Navigating the often tumultuous and intricate waters of leadership effectively necessitates a compass that is deeply rooted in self-awareness. Consider the advantage of possessing a meticulously detailed map of your own internal landscape, a tool that provides guidance for every decision you make and each interaction you engage in. Self-assessment tools play a vital role in this journey of self-discovery and understanding. Take, for instance, the Myers-Briggs Type Indicator (MBTI), a widely recognized tool that offers profound insights into personality types. This indicator provides valuable information on how you perceive the world and make decisions, dissecting aspects of your personality to identify whether you are more introverted or extroverted, sensing or intuitive, thinking or feeling, judging or perceiving. Such revelations can shed light on why you react in certain ways across various situations, thus enabling you to leverage your inherent tendencies to your advantage while remaining cautious of potential blind spots that might otherwise have gone unnoticed.

Assessments of emotional intelligence serve to further enrich this landscape of self-awareness by evaluating your capacity to adeptly manage emotions and nourish relationships. These assessments delve into several important factors such as emotional awareness and empathy, providing a broad snapshot of your current levels of emotional intelligence. With this insightful knowledge in hand, you can identify specific areas ripe for growth and development, ultimately enhancing your capability to lead with a blend of empathy and clarity.

Reflection exercises provide yet another valuable avenue for nurturing and cultivating self-awareness. Among these, journaling prompts prove particularly effective for self-discovery, offering a safe and reflective space to delve into personal thoughts and feelings devoid of judgment. Consider engaging with prompts like "What am I feeling right now?" or "How did I manage a challenging situation today?" This practice is instrumental in encouraging introspection, allowing you to unearth recurring patterns in your behavior and emotions. Mindfulness meditation acts as an ideal companion to journaling by fostering a non-judgmental awareness of the here and now. Through the committed practice of meditation, you learn to observe thoughts and emotions without becoming entangled in them, creating precious space for calm reflection and insightful understanding.

Feedback is of paramount importance in the development of self-awareness, offering fresh and diverse perspectives that might have otherwise eluded your notice. Tools such as 360-degree feedback provide a comprehensive view of your behaviors as perceived by peers, supervisors, and subordinates. This holistic approach can reveal significant discrepancies between your self-perception and how others view you, shedding light on areas that may require improvement that are often not immediately obvious. Actively seeking constructive criticism from trusted colleagues further enriches this process. Engaging them in conversations about specific situations where they observed strengths or potential areas for growth can offer valuable reflections, mirroring aspects of yourself that may warrant attention or celebration.

Ongoing practices of self-monitoring ensure that self-awareness remains an active pursuit, rather than a singular endeavor or occasion. Daily self-check-ins serve as simple yet effective tools for sustaining this awareness. Set aside a few intentional minutes each day to ponder questions like "How am I feeling emotionally?" or

"What goals did I achieve today?" These reflective moments keep you attuned to your emotional state and ongoing progress.

Mindful awareness logs represent another thoughtful method for closely tracking emotional states over time. By recording triggers, reactions, and subsequent outcomes, you create a detailed archive of emotional patterns that might influence decision-making or interactions with others. This log transforms into an invaluable resource for identifying trends, addressing them, and implementing strategies to manage emotions more constructively.

Interactive Element: Guided Reflection Exercise

Choose a quiet space where you will be free from disturbances. Set a timer for 10 minutes and focus intently on the prompt: "Reflect on a recent situation that challenged your self-awareness. What emotions did it evoke? How did you respond?" Allow your thoughts to flow freely onto the page without restriction, capturing insights candidly and without judgment. Once the time concludes, review your reflections attentively to identify any emerging themes or revelations that might offer further insight into your self-awareness.

These exercises for enhancing self-awareness offer practical and effective pathways for growth in leadership and personal development. By embracing these science-based practices, you garner a deeper understanding of yourself and how you engage with others. With every step taken towards greater self-awareness, you are empowered to lead with authenticity and empathy, fostering environments where trust, collaboration, and mutual respect naturally flourish.

EMPATHY MAPPING FOR EFFECTIVE LEADERSHIP

Navigating the complexities of leadership requires more than just strategic thinking, it demands a deep understanding of those you lead. Enter empathy mapping, a tool that helps you step into the shoes of your team, capturing their thoughts, emotions, and behaviors in a structured manner. Unlike traditional empathy exercises, which might rely on intuitive guesses, empathy mapping breaks down perceptions into clear components, offering a more detailed view. An empathy map typically consists of four quadrants: what the person says, thinks, feels, and does. This structured approach allows you to gather insights not just from verbal communication but also from unspoken cues and behaviors. So instead of guessing what your team might need or feel, you can use this tool to systematically understand their perspectives.

Creating an empathy map involves several thoughtful steps. Start by identifying the individual or group whose perspective you want to explore. Gather data through observations, interviews, or surveys, anything that provides insight into their experience. As you fill out each quadrant of the map, don't just focus on what's apparent; delve into the subtleties. What might they be reluctant to say? What fears or hopes could influence their actions? This deeper dive helps you build a comprehensive picture of their mindset. In leadership, use empathy maps to understand the dynamics within your team better. Perhaps one team member feels undervalued, leading to disengagement. By mapping their emotional landscape, you can address these issues proactively, tailoring your approach to meet their needs more effectively.

Empathy mapping can significantly enhance communication and decision-making. When you understand the motivations and challenges your team faces, you're better equipped to make informed decisions that align with their needs. This process transforms how you communicate; it's no longer just about relaying information but about fostering an environment where everyone feels heard and valued. By embracing diverse perspectives highlighted through empathy maps, you're more likely to find creative solutions to problems. Diverse viewpoints often lead to richer discussions and more innovative outcomes.

Developing greater empathy in leadership goes beyond just using tools, it involves honing specific skills and adopting particular mindsets. Active listening is crucial here. It's not merely about hearing words but understanding the intent and emotions behind them. Practice this by truly focusing on the speaker without planning your response while they talk. Validate their feelings with acknowledgments like "I can see why you feel that way," which reinforces trust and openness.

Engaging in perspective-taking exercises can further cultivate empathy. Imagine yourself in your team member's position, consider their daily challenges and aspirations. This mental shift helps break down your biases and assumptions, leading to more compassionate leadership. When you actively seek to understand rather than judge, you create a culture where team members feel appreciated for who they are.

Empathy mapping isn't just a theoretical exercise, it has real-world benefits that can transform your leadership style. Consider a team struggling with low morale due to recent changes in the company. By using empathy maps, you uncover underlying concerns: fears about job security or frustrations with new processes. Armed with this information, you can communicate more effectively about these changes, addressing worries head-on and involving the team in crafting solutions.

Ultimately, empathy mapping empowers leaders to connect on a human level with their teams, bridging gaps that might otherwise go unnoticed. It's about seeing beyond the surface to understand the heart of what drives people, both their fears and their motivations and using that understanding to lead in a way that is both effective and humane. As you embrace these techniques, you'll find yourself fostering stronger relationships within your team, built on trust and mutual respect.

DECISION-MAKING WITH EMOTIONAL INTELLIGENCE

In the whirlwind of decision-making, emotional intelligence acts as your steady anchor, balancing the scales between logic and emotion. Emotions have a knack for stealthily infiltrating our choices, influencing outcomes in significant ways that we might not always consciously realize. Acknowledging emotional biases becomes a critical skill that one must diligently cultivate, allowing for the differentiation between a meaningful gut feeling and an emotional impulse that might inadvertently lead you astray. Picture the intricate scenario where a major business decision looms large and imposes itself, logic might steadfastly dictate one specific path while your emotions powerfully pull you in an entirely different direction. In these complex moments, emotional intelligence steps in to aid you in weighing these elements with careful consideration, ensuring that neither logic nor emotion dominates without receiving its due evaluation and scrutiny.

To seamlessly integrate emotional intelligence into your decision-making process, consider employing the straightforward and effective STOP model: Stop, Think, Observe, Proceed. It's a deceptively simple yet remarkably effective strategy. When faced with a complex decision, initiate the process by pausing, give yourself the invaluable gift of space and time to step back from immediate knee-jerk reactions. Then, engage in deep introspection to think conscientiously about the emotions at play, and what subtle messages they might be conveying to you. Observing involves systematically considering the situation from various multifaceted perspectives, fully embracing both the hard facts and the nuanced feelings involved. Finally, proceed confidently with a decision that harmoniously aligns with both your logical analysis and emotional understanding. This structured approach diligently helps to prevent hasty decisions driven singularly by emotion or cold logic alone.

Managing emotions during high-stakes decisions is crucial. Contrary to misconceptions, emotional regulation is not about suppressing genuine feelings but instead is about comprehending and channeling them constructively in a positive manner. Techniques such as deep breathing exercises or brief meditation sessions can significantly calm the mind, creating a serene and clearer mental space for carefully evaluating various options. In moments rife with stress, these practices become invaluable tools for maintaining a sense of balance and perspective. They allow you to address the decision at hand with a clear mind and a steady heart, ensuring that every choice made is considered, deliberate, and well thought out.

Emotional intelligence also plays a pivotal role in ethical decision-making, guiding leaders to act consistently with integrity and fairness. When faced with formidable ethical dilemmas, leaders with high EI can navigate complexities by considering not just immediate needs, but the broader impact of their decisions on stakeholders and the entire organization. Emotional intelligence fosters empathy, skillfully enabling leaders to appreciate diverse perspectives and understand the repercussions of their choices extending far beyond immediate outcomes. This insight often leads to more equitable, fair-minded solutions that resonate with deeply held moral principles.

Consider a vivid example of a leader who encounters an ethical challenge in resource allocation between departments. With heightened emotional intelligence, she is able to keenly empathize with each department's distinct needs and constraints while thoughtfully assessing the potential outcomes for the entire organization as a whole. This empathetic approach empowers her to arrive at a solution that maximizes resources equitably, effectively maintaining trust and morale across all teams.

Textual Element: Case Study on Ethical Decision-Making

Reflect on a leader universally known for their ethical decision-making profoundly grounded in emotional intelligence, someone whose choices have persistently upheld integrity and fairness. Consider how they deliberately approached ethical dilemmas and the palpable impact they had on their team or organization. Carefully write down insights gleaned from their approach that you can incorporate into your own decision-making processes, creating a virtuous cycle of informed, principled decisions.

In wrapping up this chapter on enhancing emotional intelligence and self-awareness, it is essential to remember that these skills are far more than mere tools; they are profound, transformative forces in leadership. They guide you to make decisions that are effective and principled, foster environments of trust, respect, and mutual understanding. As you step triumphantly into the next chapter, we'll explore how these foundational skills robustly support effective delegation and team empowerment, key elements in driving forward both personal and professional growth. This holistic approach not only nurtures the individuals within the organization but also steers the collective vision towards success.

UNLOCK THE POWER OF LEADERSHIP

"Leadership is hard to define and good leadership even harder. But if you can get people to follow you to the ends of the earth, you are a great leader."

— *INDRA NOOYI (FORMER CEO OF PEPSICO)*

Your opinion is powerful!

By sharing your thoughts on '**Leadership For Women**', you're not just reflecting on your own journey, you're giving others the courage and inspiration to begin theirs.

If this book has helped you gain a better understanding of your current Leadership skills and your plans for growth and development, your story could be the light that someone else needs to make a change. Every review is a ripple that reaches someone who is ready to grow, succeed and thrive.

Why Your Review Matters:

- **Inspire Others:** Your feedback could be the nudge someone needs to invest in themselves and their future.
- **Share Your Wins:** When you highlight what worked for you, you help others see that success is within their reach.
- **Support the Mission:** Your review spreads the message of the benefits of *Emotional Intelligence* to more people around the world.

How to Write a Review:

1. **Be Honest:** Share your favorite parts, key takeaways, or how the book made a difference in your life.
2. **Keep It Simple:** A few sentences about what you loved is all it takes to make an impact.
3. **Post It Online:** Reviews on Amazon or Goodreads are the best way to help others discover this guide.

We love helping others and hope you will do the same. Thank you!

Freedom Publications: 'Your Partner in Personal Growth and Success'.

Scan the QR code to leave your review:

7

RESILIENCE AND ADAPTABILITY IN LEADERSHIP

BUILDING RESILIENCE: BOUNCING BACK FROM SETBACKS

When a tree sways in the wind, its flexibility prevents it from breaking, allowing it to withstand storms. This image captures the essence of resilience, a vital trait in leadership. Resilience is the capacity to withstand challenges and recover quickly from setbacks. For leaders, it's not just an asset but a necessity. The ability to bounce back from difficulties sets resilient leaders apart. They face obstacles with determination and use these experiences as stepping stones for growth. This is crucial for career longevity, ensuring that setbacks fuel progress rather than stall it.

Resilient leaders share specific attributes. They possess tenacity, embracing challenges as opportunities for learning and development. They maintain a positive outlook, focusing on solutions rather than problems. By fostering a growth mindset, they remain adaptive and open to change, which is essential in today's fast-paced world. Such leaders also demonstrate strong emotional intelligence, effectively managing stress and maintaining composure under pressure. This combination of traits enables them to navigate complexities with poise and confidence.

To build resilience, one can employ several techniques. Cognitive restructuring is a powerful tool for reframing challenges. It involves altering negative thought patterns and viewing setbacks as temporary and solvable rather than insurmountable. By identifying irrational beliefs and replacing them with rational ones, you gain control over your emotional responses. Visualization techniques are also effective. Picture positive outcomes, and imagine yourself overcoming obstacles with ease. This mental rehearsal boosts confidence and prepares you for real-world challenges, making success feel attainable.

Stories of resilient leaders offer valuable insights into overcoming adversity. Consider a female CEO who faced financial difficulties when launching her startup. Instead of succumbing to despair, she viewed the situation as a learning opportunity. She adjusted her business strategy, sought mentorship, and persevered despite the odds. Her resilience paid off, leading to eventual success that inspired her team and peers alike. Another example is a tech leader who encountered repeated failures in product development. Rather than giving up, she embraced each setback as a lesson, refining her approach until achieving breakthrough innovation.

These narratives underscore the importance of resilience in leadership. Each setback becomes a chance to learn, adapt, and grow stronger, reinforcing the idea that failure is not the end but a part of the journey toward success.

Exercise: Cultivating a Resilient Mindset

Gratitude journaling is an effective exercise for maintaining perspective during challenging times. Each day, write down three things you are grateful for, no matter how small. This practice shifts focus from problems to positives, fostering a mindset of abundance rather than scarcity. Additionally, incorporate stress management techniques into your routine. Deep breathing exercises or meditation can help calm the mind and reduce anxiety, enabling you to approach challenges with clarity.

Resilience isn't a trait you're born with; it's a skill you develop over time. It involves embracing failure as a teacher rather than an adversary. By adopting these practices and learning from those who have triumphed over adversity, you too can cultivate resilience that empowers you to lead with strength and determination.

In your pursuit of leadership excellence, remember that resilience is your ally. It transforms setbacks into stepping stones and challenges into opportunities for growth. Embrace this capacity to adapt and recover, knowing that each test strengthens your resolve and enhances your ability to lead effectively in any circumstance.

DEVELOPING ADAPTABILITY IN DYNAMIC ENVIRONMENTS

Adaptability is like a sail that adjusts with changing winds, keeping your leadership steady in dynamic environments. It's not just about reacting to change; it's about anticipating it, adjusting strategies, and maintaining forward momentum. In today's fast-paced world, adaptability isn't optional, it's crucial. Leaders who are adaptable possess a few key characteristics that set them apart. They are open-minded, willing to embrace new ideas, and flexible in their approaches. They thrive on change instead of fearing it, using it as a catalyst for innovation. This mindset allows them to guide their teams through transitions smoothly, ensuring that performance remains unaffected or even improves.

Adaptable leaders positively impact team performance. When leaders adjust to new circumstances, they inspire their teams to do the same. This trickle-down effect fosters an environment of agility and responsiveness. Teams become more collaborative, ready to tackle challenges with creativity rather than resistance. By embracing adaptability, you empower your team to meet shifting demands with confidence, ultimately driving success in unpredictable landscapes.

To enhance adaptability, a growth mindset is invaluable. This mindset rooted in the belief that abilities can be developed through dedication and hard work encourages continuous learning and resilience. Embracing this perspective helps you view change as an opportunity rather than a threat. Scenario planning is another effective strategy. By envisioning various future scenarios and preparing for them, you become more agile in responding to unexpected events. This preparation involves identifying potential challenges and developing flexible strategies that can be adapted as circumstances evolve.

Curiosity plays a pivotal role in fostering adaptability. It drives continuous learning and encourages you to explore new possibilities. A curious leader is always asking questions, seeking to understand rather than simply accept the status quo. This mindset not only keeps you informed but also inspires your team to adopt a culture of inquiry. Encouraging curiosity within your team means fostering an environment where questions are welcomed and innovation thrives. When curiosity is part of the organizational culture, it leads to creative problem-solving and a deeper understanding of challenges.

Practical tools can further enhance adaptability. Role-playing exercises offer a safe space to practice handling unexpected situations. These simulations allow you to experiment with different approaches and receive feedback in a low-stakes environment. By rehearsing various scenarios, you build confidence in your ability to navigate real-life challenges. Journaling prompts also promote flexible thinking. Regularly reflecting on experiences encourages you to consider alternative perspectives and solutions. This practice trains your mind to think beyond conventional boundaries and embrace innovative approaches when faced with change.

Interactive Element: Journaling Prompt for Adaptability

Reflect on a recent change in your work environment. What was your initial reaction? How did you adapt? Write down three alternative strategies you could have employed. Consider how these different approaches might have led to varied outcomes.

Through these methods, you develop the skills needed to adapt seamlessly to new circumstances. Adaptability becomes second nature, guiding you through shifts with ease and assurance. The ever-evolving nature of today's professional landscape demands leaders who can pivot swiftly and effectively. By cultivating adaptability, you're not only preparing yourself for the unknown but also empowering your team to thrive amidst uncertainty.

Adaptability isn't a static skill but a dynamic one that evolves as you grow and encounter new challenges. It's about remaining open to transformation, continuously learning, and leading with a mindset that embraces change as an integral part of progress. As you navigate the complexities of leadership, remember that adaptability is your ally a powerful tool that enables you to steer confidently through any storm life may throw your way.

LEADING THROUGH UNCERTAINTY AND CHANGE

Navigating the unpredictable waters of today's world is no small feat for any leader. The challenges of steering a team through uncertain times are multifaceted. One of the biggest hurdles is managing team morale. When uncertainty looms, anxiety can ripple through your group, affecting productivity and engagement. It's crucial to keep spirits up, even when the path ahead isn't clear. Balancing risk and opportunity is another tricky task. You need to weigh potential benefits against the pitfalls, often without all the information you'd like. This balancing act requires a keen sense of judgment and a steady hand to guide your team through the murkiness of uncertainty.

Effective leadership during change involves more than just keeping the ship afloat; it means setting a course that inspires confidence and trust. Communicating a clear vision becomes paramount. A well-articulated direction gives your team something tangible to hold onto amidst the chaos. Implementing change management frameworks can provide structure to these tumultuous periods. These frameworks offer a roadmap for navigating transitions, ensuring your team remains aligned and focused on common goals. They highlight the steps necessary for successful adaptation, allowing you to manage resources efficiently while minimizing disruptions.

Open communication is the lifeline during these times. Transparency fosters trust, which is essential when navigating unknown terrain. Encourage an environment where dialogue flows freely, and ideas are exchanged without judgment. Techniques for fostering open dialogue include active listening sessions and feedback loops where team members feel heard and valued. Regular updates and check-ins are vital for maintaining momentum. These touchpoints reassure your team that they're not navigating this alone and that you're in it together, facing challenges head-on.

Equally important is the emotional support you provide as a leader. Change can be stressful, and acknowledging this reality is crucial. Building a culture of empathy within your team creates an environment where members feel understood and supported. Offering resources for stress management, such as mindfulness workshops or access to mental health professionals, shows your commitment to their well-being. By prioritizing emotional support, you empower your team to handle change with resilience, knowing they have a safety net to fall back on.

Strategies for Sustaining Momentum During Challenges

Maintaining momentum in the face of adversity requires strategic foresight and a proactive approach. Common challenges to sustaining progress include resource limitations and constraints that can stifle creativity and innovation. Team burnout is another significant concern; prolonged periods of high stress and pressure can lead to dips in morale and productivity. Addressing these issues head-on is essential for keeping your team energized and focused on their objectives.

To sustain momentum, consider setting short-term, achievable goals that provide a sense of accomplishment and forward movement. These milestones act as stepping stones, maintaining motivation by breaking larger objectives into manageable tasks. Celebrating small victories along the way boosts morale, reminding your team of their progress and contributions.

Recognition of effort goes a long way in reinforcing commitment and dedication.

Your role as a leader in sustaining momentum is pivotal. Leading by example demonstrates the behavior you wish to see in your team, whether it's maintaining a positive attitude or displaying resilience in the face of setbacks. Encouraging collaboration fosters a sense of unity, allowing team members to draw strength from each other during challenging times. Open channels of communication promote trust, ensuring everyone feels involved in the journey.

For long-term success amidst challenges, continuous learning opportunities are key. Encourage your team to engage in professional development activities that expand their skill sets and keep them adaptable in changing environments. Regular reflection on strategies ensures they remain relevant and effective, allowing for timely adjustments as needed. By fostering a culture of growth and adaptability, you equip your team with the tools they need to thrive despite obstacles.

Leadership during uncertain times demands more than just strategic acumen; it requires empathy, communication, and unwavering support for your team. By addressing these challenges with clarity and purpose, you pave the way for success even when the road ahead is unclear.

STRATEGIES FOR SUSTAINING MOMENTUM DURING CHALLENGES

In the ever-evolving and dynamic landscape of leadership, maintaining momentum during challenging times can feel akin to the daunting task of attempting to keep a fire burning amidst a torrential downpour. Common and recurrent obstacles that leaders frequently encounter in this unpredictable journey often include an array of resource limitations and constraints. More specifically, these may manifest themselves in various troubling forms such as unexpected budget cuts, a frustrating reduction in manpower, or even the seemingly insurmountable shortages in time. All of these factors can seriously impede progress, stalling initiatives and rendering long-term goals ever so elusive. In such conditions, it's not uncommon for leaders to feel as though they are running in place without ever gaining ground. Compounding this problem is the pervasive challenge of team burnout and dips in morale, which are particularly insidious. Prolonged exposure to stress and the continuous demands placed on the team can siphon away even the strongest currents of enthusiasm, leaving your committed team feeling overburdened, overworked, and undervalued. When energy levels plummet to these low points, the consequence is often a tangible reduction in productivity and engagement, further obstructing forward momentum.

To effectively counter these formidable challenges, embracing the tactic of setting short-term, achievable goals emerges as an incredibly effective strategy. Breaking down colossal, overwhelming projects into smaller, manageable tasks provides clarity and direction, endowing your team with specific targets that cultivate a sense of accomplishment. Each completed task functions as an essential stepping stone, reinforcing confidence and stoking the fires of motivation. Celebrating small victories, no matter how modest, is equally critical. Whether it's the simple act of acknowledging individual efforts or celebrating team achievements, these moments of recognition can significantly boost morale and reinforce the intrinsic value of their efforts. Small wins serve as powerful reminders that progress is being made, even when the road ahead appears daunting and unending. These celebrations rekindle passion and commitment, infusing your team with vital energy needed to sustain momentum through times of trial.

As a leader standing at the helm, your role in sustaining this momentum is absolutely pivotal. By leading through your example, you set the tone and establish the cultural ethos for your entire team. The attitudes and behaviors you exhibit have a profound influence on those around you, sometimes in ways you might not immediately realize. Maintaining a positive outlook, even in the most adverse of situations, is a testament to resilience and serves to inspire others to adopt a similar perspective. Encouraging collaboration and fostering teamwork substantially enhances this dynamic, creating a synergistic environment where everyone inherently feels both valued and included. This inclusivity harnesses the collective strengths of the group, enabling the team to creatively and effectively overcome the obstacles they face. Collaboration not only spurs innovation by merging diverse ideas and perspectives, but it also strengthens interpersonal bonds, creating a robust supportive network that propels the team forward, even in the toughest times.

Techniques for ensuring long-term success amidst challenges necessitate a forward-thinking approach, grounded in foresight and adaptability. Continuous learning and development opportunities keep your team actively engaged and innately adaptable. Encouraging them to consistently expand their skill sets not only ensures they're equipped to adeptly handle evolving demands but also deepens their commitment to growth. This dedication to personal and professional development fosters a pervasive culture of excellence and prepares your team to surmount future challenges with confidence. Regular reflection and the adaptation of strategies are equally crucial. Taking the time to thoughtfully assess what's working versus what necessitates adjustment ensures your ability to stay both agile and responsive. This iterative process guards against mere reactivity, empowering you to proactively shape your path in an ever-changing environment.

In wrapping up this chapter, it becomes exceedingly clear that sustaining momentum in leadership does not revolve around the impossible goal of avoiding challenges altogether. Instead, it involves embracing these challenges head-on with strategic foresight, determination, and a confident mindset. By understanding the common obstacles you will likely face and employing practical, nuanced strategies designed to bolster resolve, you can maintain pivotal energy and focus even when adversity threatens to overwhelm. Remember, leadership is as much about guiding others towards collective success as it is about facilitating your own personal growth. As we turn the page to the next chapter, we will delve into how astute decision-making and effective delegation play crucial roles in leveraging these strategic insights for sustained, continued success.

8

INCLUSIVE LEADERSHIP AND DIVERSITY

EMBRACING DIVERSE LEADERSHIP STYLES

The landscape of leadership isn't monochrome, it thrives on a symphony of different approaches and methodologies, each resonating with unique strengths and nuances. Transformational leaders, for instance, are the visionaries who lift the veil on possibilities, motivating and propelling their teams toward reaching heights previously believed unattainable. They inspire innovation through aspirational goals and emerging concepts. In stark contrast, transactional leaders bring stability and clarity, anchoring their teams with well-defined roles and incentivized structure, ensuring that the gears of organizational machinery work seamlessly and efficiently.

Consider the democratic leader, who opens the floor for dialogue and input, cherishing the collective wisdom of the team. This leadership style fosters an ethos of inclusion and collaboration, where every member feels valued and engaged. In the realm of laissez-faire leadership, trust is paramount. Such leaders hand over the reins to their team, believing in their autonomy and ability to self-direct, stepping in only when necessary to provide guidance or support. This can result in an empowered team that is motivated to carve out innovative paths and take initiative towards achieving common goals.

The tapestry of leadership styles offers a rich array of benefits, especially when differences are harmoniously integrated. Picture a scenario where a company is confronting a daunting market challenge. Leaders with varied methodologies, transformational, transactional, and democratic, come together to form a council of diverse wisdom. The transformational leaders spark novel ideas while the transactional ones establish actionable metrics to navigate through challenges. Democratic leaders widen the circle for contributions, tapping into the collective intelligence and unleashing a torrent of solutions that carry the company forward. This synergy vividly illustrates how an eclectic mix of leadership styles not only enhances team dynamics but accelerates success.

In order to appreciate and cultivate diverse leadership strategies within your own team, initiating leadership style assessments can be incredibly beneficial. These diagnostics reveal personal strengths and preferences of individuals, providing a clearer picture of how differing styles can mutually enhance each other. By fostering cross-style mentorship programs, teams create a learning environment where members with contrasting leadership traits can exchange insights and grow from one another. This nurtures understanding and opens pathways to personal and professional development.

Leadership in diverse teams requires a chameleon-like adaptability. Adjusting your leadership style in response to team dynamics does not denote weakness; rather, it showcases a profound understanding of your workforce's differing motivations and needs. For example, a seasoned professional may appreciate the independence afforded by laissez-faire leadership, thriving with room for creativity and initiative. Conversely, newcomers might find comfort and stability in the clear guidelines and predictability offered by a transactional approach.

Consider, for example, the story of a leader who navigated the turbulent waters of a quickly shifting market landscape. Initially, she adhered to a transactional leadership approach, focusing heavily on structure and results orientation. However, recognizing that her team needed a revitalized approach to unleash creativity and responsiveness, she embraced transformational strategies. This pivot not only birthed a renewed enthusiasm and engagement among team members but also allowed her leadership skills to evolve, proving the power of adaptability.

Interactive Element: Leadership Style Reflection

Take this moment to delve deeper into your own leadership style. Ponder these guiding questions: What leadership style resonates with you the most? In what contexts or situations has it propelled your success? Where might flexibility and adaptability open new pathways for growth? Embrace these reflections to discover how incorporating diverse leadership styles can enhance your leadership journey and foster a more inclusive environment.

By acknowledging and weaving diverse leadership styles into your approach, you create a nurturing atmosphere where each voice is heard, respected, and valued. Leadership then transcends mere management, it evolves into a symbiotic relationship of mutual inspiration, adaptability, and collective progress, nurturing growth for both leader and team alike. As you explore these concepts further, remember that leadership is not a static position, it is a dynamic journey that invites you to inspire, adapt, and grow alongside your team.

FOSTERING AN INCLUSIVE WORK ENVIRONMENT

Creating an inclusive work environment is akin to meticulously cultivating a flourishing garden where each and every plant, irrespective of its size, shape, or hue, blossoms to its fullest potential in its own extraordinary way. This concept of inclusivity in the workplace is fundamentally about nurturing a space where individual employees feel genuinely valued, profoundly respected, and genuinely empowered to deliver their very best contributions, thereby enhancing both personal and organizational growth.

An inclusive organization is characterized by diverse representation across every hierarchical level, ensuring that opportunities for advancement are equitable and that the organizational culture celebrates differences rather than merely tolerating them. The essence of this environment is steeped in mutual respect and collaboration, where diverse voices are not solely listened to but actively sought out and integrated into the fabric of the organization. When employees experience a true sense of inclusion, engagement levels soar, employee retention is significantly bolstered, and the entire organization reaps the benefits of invigorated creativity coupled with robust innovation.

To successfully cultivate such an inclusive culture, leaders must take deliberate and substantial steps that go far beyond superficial, surface-level changes. Implementing comprehensive diversity training programs emerges as a crucial move towards this goal. These programs serve the essential purpose of raising awareness about and deepening the understanding of unconscious biases that may prevail in the workplace, ultimately fostering an environment that wholeheartedly celebrates differences. It's paramount that these programs are continuous, offering ongoing opportunities for growth, learning, and development.

Inclusive hiring practices serve as another foundational cornerstone of this endeavor. Crafting job descriptions tailored to attract a wide spectrum of candidates ensures that the talent pool is rich with diversity. At the same time, it's vital that recruitment panels themselves represent a broad array of backgrounds and perspectives. By establishing employee resource groups (ERGs), organizations create platforms where underrepresented groups can come together to share experiences, provide mutual support, and exert influence over company policies. These ERGs offer an invaluable repository of insights into the unique needs and perspectives of various communities within the workplace, facilitating a culture of understanding and empathy.

Leadership plays a pivotal and transformative role in the modeling of inclusivity. This journey begins with leaders embodying inclusive behaviors in both their words and actions. They must maintain mindfulness regarding their language, ensuring it is perpetually respectful and inclusive, while also demonstrating a profound openness to various perspectives. By actively seeking out varied viewpoints during decision-making processes, leaders guarantee that choices and solutions reflect an abundance of experiences and insights. This approach not only enriches the decision-making process but also communicates to all employees that their contributions are both significant and invaluable. Leaders should endeavor to provide platforms where every voice, regardless of its position in the hierarchy, is heard and esteemed, actively dismantling any system of hierarchies that might otherwise suppress participation from less represented groups.

Measuring inclusivity is critical to discerning how successfully an organization upholds inclusive values and identifying key areas for improvement. Inclusivity audits offer a comprehensive methodology to meticulously assess whether the workplace genuinely reflects these core values. Such audits can examine representation across different roles and departments, scrutinize promotion practices, and gather feedback from employees regarding their lived experiences within the company. Regular surveys serve as another potent tool, offering anonymous feedback from a diverse range of employee groups on their perceptions of inclusivity within the organization. Establishing these regular feedback mechanisms ensures that inclusivity remains a dynamic process, continually evolving in response to the ever-changing needs and experiences of employees.

Incorporating these strategies within a leadership framework assists in crafting a workplace where each individual truly feels they belong. Inclusivity transcends the realm of simple policies or programs; it represents a culture where diversity is celebrated as a potent strength, not merely a checkbox to be marked off. When an inclusive environment is nurtured, it invites a wealth of rich perspectives and innovative ideas that can drive both profound innovation and sustained growth. It's about creating a holistic environment where everyone feels empowered to bring their complete and authentic selves to work. In this kind of nurturing environment, individuals not only flourish but thrive, secure in the knowledge that their unique contributions are both recognized and deeply valued.

THE ROLE OF DIVERSITY IN INNOVATION AND GROWTH

Diversity acts like the secret ingredient that spices up creativity and drives innovation within organizations. Imagine a team where every member brings a unique perspective, shaped by their experiences, backgrounds, and cultures. These diverse perspectives are the lifeblood of creative solutions, pushing the boundaries of conventional thinking and sparking ideas that one-dimensional teams might overlook. When different viewpoints converge, they often lead to the development of innovative products and services that cater to a broader audience, effectively opening new avenues for growth. For instance, companies that embrace diversity tend to show higher levels of adaptability and resilience, thriving even in unpredictable markets due to their multifaceted approach to problem-solving.

Let's look at some real-world examples. Companies like Google and Apple have harnessed the power of diversity-driven innovation to stay at the forefront of technology and design. Google's commitment to diversity is evident in its array of products tailored to a global audience, each benefiting from diverse ideas and insights. Similarly, Apple's diverse workforce has played a critical role in creating inclusive products that appeal to various demographics. These companies illustrate how embracing diversity can lead to groundbreaking innovations that capture market share and enhance customer loyalty.

Beyond creativity, diversity also brings tangible economic benefits. Research consistently shows that diverse teams outperform their homogenous counterparts in profitability. A study by McKinsey & Company found that companies with diverse executive teams are more likely to have financial returns above their national industry medians. Diversity fuels market expansion by leveraging insights from varied backgrounds, enabling companies to tap into new customer segments and geographies with confidence. When team members share experiences that resonate with diverse consumers, they can identify unmet needs and develop tailored solutions that drive growth.

To capitalize on these benefits, leaders can implement strategies that actively leverage diversity for organizational growth. One effective approach is to encourage diverse idea generation sessions where team members from different backgrounds collaborate on brainstorming activities. These sessions should foster an open environment where all voices are heard and valued, allowing for the free flow of ideas without judgment. Additionally, building project teams with a mix of perspectives ensures that solutions are comprehensive and well-rounded. This diversity of thought leads to robust decision-making processes that consider multiple angles and potential outcomes.

However, managing diverse teams isn't without its challenges. Differences in communication styles, cultural norms, and expectations can sometimes lead to misunderstandings or conflicts. It's crucial for leaders to recognize these potential pitfalls and proactively address them. Conflict resolution strategies tailored to diverse teams should focus on understanding and respecting individual differences while finding common ground. Techniques like mediation and facilitated discussions can help navigate disagreements constructively, ensuring that all voices are acknowledged and valued.

Equally important is ensuring equal participation in discussions. Leaders should create an inclusive environment where everyone feels comfortable contributing their ideas. This might involve implementing structured meeting formats that allow quieter team members the opportunity to speak or utilizing digital tools that facilitate anonymous input during brainstorming sessions. By actively promoting equal participation, leaders empower their teams to harness the full spectrum of diversity and drive collective success.

In summary, embracing diversity is not just a social imperative; it's a strategic advantage that fuels innovation and growth. By actively seeking out diverse perspectives and fostering an inclusive culture, organizations can unlock new opportunities, create innovative solutions, and achieve sustainable success in today's complex business landscape.

LEADING WITH EMPATHY AND UNDERSTANDING

Leading with empathy is like skillfully navigating the nuanced complexities of human interactions, wielding a finely tuned compass that guides you through the roughest emotional seas. It demands a commitment to connecting with others on a profoundly personal level, understanding their emotions fully, and responding in a manner that is both thoughtful and intentional. Empathetic leadership transcends mere sympathy; it involves delving into the hearts and minds of others to cultivate an environment where nurturing becomes second nature.

Empathetic leaders are often seen as beacons of hope and comfort within their teams. They naturally embody qualities such as active listening, profound patience, and an authentic concern for the well-being of their teammates, qualities that are not just appreciated, but deeply revered. These leaders establish spaces where team morale is not a fleeting achievement but a sustained and flourishing ecosystem. Loyalty becomes more than a reward; it is organically and effortlessly cultivated as part of the team's culture.

Developing empathy as a leader is a journey that calls for deliberate, consistent practice and deep reflection. To begin, one must focus on refining active listening skills, a discipline that speaks volumes when practiced with sincerity. Active listening is an intricate dance where the listener does not merely hear words, but intently captures the subtle emotional undertones and unspoken intentions. This can be cultivated through exercises that encourage focused attention on what the other person is sharing, all while resisting the urge to interrupt or mentally draft a response. To truly embrace and absorb their perspective, allow yourself a moment of pause before offering a reply. Perspective-taking workshops serve as an invaluable tool in this process, offering rich scenarios in which you immerse yourself in another's reality. By doing so, you gradually dismantle preconceived notions and replace them with genuine understanding.

Empathy serves as the bedrock of trust within any team. A team that feels genuinely understood and valued is one that naturally develops trust. Historical anecdotes of leaders who have successfully bridged gaps and resolved conflicts through empathy provide valuable lessons. Consider a leader embroiled in a heated dispute, who, instead of asserting dominance, chooses to listen with an open heart and an inclusive mindset, acknowledging all viewpoints with respect. Such actions can not only defuse tension but also create a pathway to resolution that satisfies all parties involved. Techniques for empathetic conflict resolution are crucial; they involve recognizing emotions, searching for common ground, and honoring individual needs without compromising them. These approaches underscore that empathy is far from being merely a soft skill; it is a profound tool for fostering collaboration and fortifying relationships.

Leaders aspiring to weave empathy into the very fabric of their daily routines might find solace in practical tools and exercises that promise substantial growth. Empathy mapping is a particularly insightful method that aids leaders in gaining a thorough understanding of their team members' perspectives. By mapping out what individuals say, think, feel, and do, leaders can discern patterns and strategically tailor their approaches to meet the team's unique needs. Role-playing scenarios offer yet another path for development, allowing leaders to rehearse responding empathetically to a variety of situations, ensuring understanding always precedes solution-offering. These exercises not only sharpen your empathy skills but amplify your ability to genuinely connect with your team, nurturing a bond that transcends superficial interactions.

In summarizing this chapter on empathy, it becomes abundantly clear that leading with understanding is not a singular act but rather an enduring commitment to valuing the human element within every interaction. It builds bridges where previously only walls existed, reshaping the dynamics into a harmonious environment of trust and collaboration. As you venture further into this journey of personal and professional evolution, remember that empathy is the key that opens the door to deeper, more meaningful connections with those around you.

With this rich understanding of empathetic leadership, we pave the way for our next exploration. As we turn the page, we will delve into the realms of decision-making and delegation, uncovering how they empower leaders to govern with clarity and alignment to their values and vision.

9

GOAL SETTING AND ACHIEVING SUCCESS

VISION CASTING FOR PERSONAL AND PROFESSIONAL SUCCESS

Think about a time when you felt lost, unsure of your next step. Now imagine having a clear picture of where you want to be, a vision so vivid it propels you forward even when the path seems uncertain. This is the essence of vision casting, a powerful tool for creating long-term success. Unlike goal setting, which outlines specific steps to achieve an outcome, vision casting is about dreaming big and envisioning your ideal future. It's about setting the stage for your goals, providing a north star to guide every decision and action.

Vision casting isn't just a buzzword, it's a profound psychological tool. A clear vision not only inspires but also brings focus and purpose. It helps you maintain motivation during challenging times, offering a reminder of why you started. While goals break down your journey into actionable steps, a vision paints the broader picture, keeping you aligned with your deepest aspirations. This distinction is crucial in ensuring that your day-to-day actions remain connected to your bigger dreams.

Crafting a compelling vision statement involves intentional reflection. Begin by considering what truly matters to you in both personal and professional realms. What impact do you want to make? Use vision statement templates to guide this process, helping distill your thoughts into concise, powerful language. For instance, consider the visionary statements of leaders like Oprah Winfrey, whose vision of empowering others through media has driven her career. These statements act as beacons, illuminating the path ahead.

Once you have your vision statement, visualization exercises can reinforce this vision and help maintain focus. Guided visualizations are particularly effective. Set aside quiet time, close your eyes, and vividly imagine achieving your vision. What does it look like? How does it feel? Engage all your senses to make the experience as real as possible. This practice not only solidifies your commitment but also primes your mind for success.

Creating a vision board is another powerful way to keep your vision front and center. Gather images, words, and quotes that resonate with your vision and arrange them on a board where you'll see them daily. This visual representation serves as a constant reminder, sparking motivation every time you glance at it. The act of assembling a vision board itself can be transformative, helping clarify and energize your aspirations.

Interactive Element: Vision Board Creation Exercise

Collect magazines, printouts, or online images that symbolize your dreams and goals. Arrange them creatively on a board or digital platform, adding affirmations or quotes that inspire you.

Place this vision board somewhere visible to keep your aspirations alive every day.

A strong vision does more than inspire, it drives motivation and guides actions. Consider leaders like Elon Musk, whose audacious visions for space travel and renewable energy have not only transformed industries but also motivated teams to achieve what once seemed impossible. These leaders illustrate how a clear vision can steer decision-making processes, ensuring every action aligns with overarching goals.

To maintain alignment with your vision, integrate it into daily routines. Begin each day by reflecting on how your actions contribute to realizing your vision. This practice keeps you grounded and ensures that even small tasks are purposeful. Regular check-ins with yourself or a trusted mentor can also provide accountability and support in staying true to your vision.

Incorporating your vision into everyday life requires dedication but reaps significant rewards. It shapes how you approach challenges, providing clarity when faced with tough choices. Your vision becomes a compass, pointing you toward opportunities that resonate with your core values and aspirations.

By embracing vision casting, you create a roadmap that not only charts where you want to go but also enriches the journey itself. It empowers you to lead with intention and clarity, transforming dreams into reality with confidence and purpose.

SETTING SMART GOALS FOR LEADERSHIP GROWTH

Setting out on a road trip without a map or destination in mind isn't the most sensible thing to do. It might be thrilling for a moment, but eventually, being directionless becomes frustrating. This is where SMART goals come into play, offering you a roadmap for success. SMART is an acronym for Specific, Measurable, Achievable, Relevant, and Time-bound. It serves as a robust framework for setting goals that are not only clear but also actionable. Each element of the SMART criteria plays a crucial role in shaping goals that propel you toward growth. Specific goals eliminate ambiguity, providing a clear target. Measurable criteria allow you to track progress, ensuring accountability. Achievable goals remain realistic within your resources and capabilities, preventing discouragement. Relevance ensures alignment with broader objectives, keeping you focused on what truly matters. Finally, setting a timeline instills urgency, encouraging action and prioritization.

Crafting SMART goals requires thoughtful reflection and clarity. Begin by identifying areas where you seek growth or change. For example, perhaps you aim to enhance your team's productivity. Instead of vaguely aspiring to "improve productivity," specify how much you want to increase it by and within what timeframe. A SMART goal might read: "Increase team productivity by 15% over the next quarter by implementing weekly progress tracking and feedback sessions." This goal is specific in its target, measurable with its percentage increase, achievable through clear actions, relevant to team success, and time-bound with a quarterly deadline.

As you set your SMART goals, consider using tools and techniques to monitor progress and stay on track. Goal-tracking apps such as Asana or Trello offer platforms to organize tasks and deadlines, providing visual representations of your journey. These tools help break down larger goals into manageable steps, making the path forward clearer. Additionally, incorporating weekly and monthly progress reviews can be instrumental in maintaining momentum. Use templates to assess achievements and identify areas for adjustment, fostering a cycle of continuous improvement.

The impact of SMART goals on leadership development is profound. They act as catalysts for growth, transforming aspirations into tangible outcomes. Consider leaders who have achieved remarkable success through this approach. Take, for example, a female entrepreneur who launched her startup by setting clear milestones for product development and market entry, using feedback to refine her strategy along the way. Her story highlights how SMART goals can turn ambitious visions into reality.

Adjusting goals based on feedback and results is crucial to maintaining their effectiveness. As you progress, remain open to insights from peers or mentors, allowing their perspectives to inform necessary adjustments. Perhaps an initial goal seemed attainable but revealed unforeseen challenges; adapting it ensures continued progress without the burden of unrealistic expectations. This flexibility allows goals to evolve in response to changing circumstances while staying aligned with your overarching vision.

By integrating SMART goals into your leadership practice, you cultivate a mindset of purposefulness and direction. Each goal achieved is a step forward in your development as a leader, building confidence and competence along the way. The clarity provided by SMART criteria empowers you to focus energy on what truly matters, driving meaningful progress in your career or business. This structured approach not only enhances personal growth but also inspires those around you, fostering an environment of shared success and collaboration.

Incorporate these practices into your daily routine with intentionality and commitment. As you set new goals or revisit existing ones, allow the principles of specificity, measurability, achievability, relevance, and time-bound action to guide you. Embrace the challenges that come with goal-setting as opportunities for learning and growth. Celebrate each milestone reached as evidence of your dedication and resilience.

Let these techniques for setting SMART goals become an integral part of your leadership toolkit, tools that empower you to navigate complexities with clarity and confidence. Whether stepping into new roles or refining your current position, these strategies offer a roadmap for achieving success on your terms.

As you explore the potential of SMART goals in your leadership journey, remember that every goal set is a step toward realizing your aspirations. Embrace this approach with enthusiasm and determination, knowing that each goal brings you closer to the leader you aspire to be.

ALIGNING GOALS WITH PERSONAL VALUES

If you were driving down a highway, and each exit represented a different opportunity, without a clear understanding of where you're headed, every exit seems enticing, yet none truly feels right. This is what setting goals without aligning them with your personal values can feel like, directionless and unfulfilling. By understanding the connection between values and goal setting, you ensure that each step you take in your professional and personal life feels resonant and purposeful. When goals align with your core values, the journey toward achieving them becomes not only rewarding but also deeply satisfying.

To align your goals with your values, start by identifying what truly matters to you. Take time to explore your personal values through exercises designed to uncover them. Reflect on moments when you felt most alive or fulfilled. What values were you honoring in those times? Was it creativity, integrity, or perhaps compassion? Write these down, creating a list of guiding principles that shape who you are. This exercise not only clarifies your values but also provides a foundation for setting meaningful goals that reflect who you are at your core.

Consider examples of value-driven goals to inspire your process. Let's say one of your core values is sustainability. A value-aligned goal might involve leading an initiative at work to reduce waste or implement eco-friendly practices. This goal not only advances your career but also satisfies your personal commitment to environmental stewardship, making the achievement feel richer and more rewarding.

Once you've identified your values, prioritize goals that resonate most deeply with them. Decision-making frameworks like the Eisenhower Matrix can help. This tool categorizes tasks by urgency and importance, allowing you to focus on goals that align with your values while avoiding those that might conflict with them. By consistently choosing value-aligned paths, you maintain integrity in your pursuits.

Avoiding conflicts in goal setting is essential for staying true to your values. When faced with opportunities that seem enticing but clash with your principles, remind yourself of the bigger picture. A lucrative job offer that contradicts your dedication to work-life balance might seem tempting, but ultimately, it could lead to dissatisfaction. Techniques such as scenario planning can help anticipate potential conflicts and prepare responses that uphold your values.

Leaders who align their goals with personal values often experience heightened motivation and satisfaction. Consider the story of a female entrepreneur who prioritized innovation and social impact. Her company thrived not just financially but also in making meaningful contributions to society. This alignment fueled her passion and perseverance, illustrating how staying true to values can yield both personal and professional success.

Maintaining focus on value-aligned goals requires vigilance and dedication. Regularly revisit your goals to ensure they remain true to your evolving values. As life changes, so too might your priorities, what mattered deeply last year may shift in significance today. Techniques for maintaining this alignment include setting aside time for reflection and conducting periodic reviews of both values and goals.

Tools for reflecting on values and goals are invaluable in this ongoing process. Engage in journaling prompts designed to stimulate introspection and clarity. Questions like "What am I most proud of this month?" or "How did I honor my values this week?" encourage thoughtful consideration of how well you're living in accordance with your principles. Through these reflections, you gain insights into where adjustments might be necessary.

Journaling Prompt: Values Reflection

Take a moment to write about a recent decision or action that felt particularly fulfilling or challenging. What values were at play? Did they guide or conflict with the outcome? How can these insights inform future goal setting?

As your journey unfolds, remember that aligning goals with personal values is not a one-time task but an evolving practice that adapts as you grow. It's about creating harmony between who you are and what you aspire to achieve, ensuring that every goal pursued is a step toward a life rich with purpose and fulfillment. By continually aligning actions with core values, you cultivate a sense of authenticity and satisfaction that permeates all aspects of life.

CREATING A STRATEGIC PLAN FOR SUCCESS

Strategic planning is more than just a buzzword, it's the compass that guides your long-term ambitions. Unlike spontaneous actions or impromptu decisions, a strategic plan lays out a detailed blueprint for achieving your goals, both personal and professional. It's about looking at the big picture, setting priorities, and allocating resources effectively. Think of it as your personal GPS, providing direction and helping you stay on course even when detours arise. The elements of an effective strategic plan include clear objectives, actionable steps, timelines, and evaluation methods. Each component plays a crucial role in transforming broad aspirations into tangible achievements.

Creating a personal strategic plan involves intentional reflection and structured methodology. Start by identifying your core aspirations. What do you want to achieve in the next year, five years, or even a decade? Use strategic planning templates to organize your thoughts and break down complex goals into manageable tasks. These templates help create a roadmap with clear milestones and checkpoints, ensuring you remain aligned with your overall vision. Drawing inspiration from industry leaders can also be invaluable. Consider how figures like Sheryl Sandberg or Indra Nooyi have leveraged strategic planning to navigate their careers. Their plans often emphasize adaptability, focusing on both long-term goals and immediate actions needed to reach them.

Once your strategic plan is in place, implementing it requires dedication and flexibility. Setting milestones and timelines is crucial to maintain momentum. Milestones act as mini-goals, providing opportunities to celebrate progress and reassess strategies. Techniques such as backward planning can be effective. Start with your end goal in mind and work backward to determine the steps needed to get there. Regular evaluations are essential for iterating on your plan. Life is unpredictable, and being open to adjustments ensures your plan remains relevant and achievable. Periodic reviews allow you to reflect on what's working, what isn't, and how you can pivot to stay on track.

Accountability plays a pivotal role in strategic planning. Without it, even the best-laid plans can falter. Consider building accountability partnerships with trusted colleagues or mentors. These partnerships foster mutual support and encouragement, providing a sounding board for ideas and challenges. Sharing your progress with someone invested in your success not only reinforces commitment but also offers external perspectives that can enhance your approach. Utilizing accountability tools and platforms like Trello or Asana can further bolster this process. These tools help track progress in real-time, visualize tasks, and set reminders for upcoming deadlines.

The journey of strategic planning is ongoing, requiring patience and persistence. It's about laying the groundwork for lasting success, ensuring that each step taken is purposeful and aligned with your broader objectives. By integrating strategic planning into your routine, you equip yourself with the tools needed to navigate complexities with confidence and clarity. This process isn't just about reaching a destination; it's about creating a fulfilling path that resonates with your values and aspirations.

As we conclude this chapter on goal setting and achieving success, remember that a strategic plan is more than just a document, it's an evolving guide that adapts as you grow and change. Embrace this tool with enthusiasm and dedication, knowing that each strategic decision brings you closer to the leader you aspire to be.

In our next chapter, we will explore the art of effective decision-making, delving into techniques that enhance leadership capabilities by ensuring choices align with strategic objectives. This seamless transition from planning to decision-making underscores the interconnected nature of leadership skills, each one building upon the other to create a cohesive, successful approach.

10

COMMUNICATION TECHNIQUES FOR IMPACT

MASTERING PUBLIC SPEAKING AND PRESENTATION SKILLS

As a leader you will often have to give talks to teams, chair meetings and give presentations to audiences of varying sizes. Standing on stage can be daunting, the spotlight warming your face, and the audience's anticipation palpable. Public speaking can feel like standing on a precipice, ready to leap into the unknown. But this leap doesn't have to be daunting. It can be exhilarating when equipped with the right tools and mindset. Public speaking is more than just talking, it's about connecting with others on a deeper level, sharing stories and insights that resonate and inspire. The core principles of effective public speaking are your map to navigate this journey. Structuring your speech with a clear beginning, middle, and end is crucial. Start by crafting a strong opening that grabs attention, perhaps a question, a startling fact, or a personal anecdote. This sets the stage for your message, drawing your audience in.

As you move into the body of your speech, clarity is key. Divide your content into digestible segments, each supporting your main point. Use examples and stories to illustrate your message, making it relatable and memorable. Conclude with a powerful closing that reinforces your message and leaves a lasting impression. This might be a call to action or a thought-provoking statement that lingers in the minds of your listeners long after you've left the stage.

Stage fright is a common hurdle for many speakers. It can feel like butterflies in your stomach have turned into stampeding elephants. But just like any challenge, it can be managed with the right techniques. Breathing exercises are your first line of defense. Before stepping on stage, take deep breaths, inhaling for four counts, holding for four, and exhaling slowly for another four. This calms your nerves and centers your thoughts.

Visualization techniques can also boost confidence. Close your eyes and picture yourself delivering a successful presentation to an audience engaged, nodding along with your points. This mental rehearsal instills confidence, making the actual event feel familiar and less intimidating.

Engaging your audience is an art form. It transforms your presentation from a monologue into a conversation. Storytelling is one of the most effective tools for engagement. By weaving narratives into your presentation, you create an emotional connection with your audience. Stories humanize data and concepts, making them more accessible and impactful.

Incorporating visual aids can also enhance engagement. Use slides with minimal text to support your points without overwhelming viewers. Images, graphs, or short videos can illustrate concepts in ways that words alone cannot. Ensure these aids are clear and relevant, enhancing rather than detracting from your message.

Crafting presentations that leave an impression requires thoughtful design and delivery. When designing slides, focus on simplicity. Each slide should convey one key idea using visuals that complement your spoken words. Avoid clutter by limiting text and using large fonts for readability.

Your body language is another powerful tool in delivering memorable presentations. It reinforces your message and conveys confidence to your audience. Stand tall with shoulders back, maintaining eye contact to build rapport. Use gestures deliberately to emphasize points but avoid distracting movements.

Interactive Element: Reflection Exercise

Identify a public speaker you admire and analyze their technique. Reflect on their use of storytelling, body language, and audience engagement. Consider how you can incorporate these elements into your own presentations.

Remember, public speaking is not about perfection, it's about connection. Each time you speak, you grow more confident and articulate, refining your style and finding your voice. Whether in a boardroom or on a stage, these techniques empower you to communicate with impact, leaving audiences inspired and eager for more.

THE ART OF PERSUASION AND INFLUENCE

Persuasion and influence, often deemed as the twin pillars of impactful leadership, serve as the intricate yet invisible forces that navigate decisions and shape actions. They transcend mere communication, steering individuals towards a shared vision or collective goal. It is crucial to differentiate persuasion from coercion or manipulation; persuasion is about instilling inspiration and motivation, encouraging others to embrace a vision with eagerness and enthusiasm. It involves skillfully presenting ideas in a manner that captivates interest, underpinning them with sound reasoning and emotional resonance to encourage voluntary acceptance. Influence advances this concept further by embedding itself within the broader tapestry of trust and respect, forming enduring imprints on others' perceptions and behaviors. True persuasion respects the agency and autonomy of those it seeks to reach, aiming for mutually beneficial outcomes and deeper understanding. This approach, grounded in sincerity and authenticity, lays the groundwork for robust relationships and lasting leadership.

For leaders aiming to master the art of persuasion, embracing key strategies that anchor interactions in integrity is essential. One such strategy is the principle of reciprocity, a timeless concept suggesting that actions or favors are often returned, thereby nurturing a cycle of goodwill and collaboration. By proactively offering value in the form of support, resources, or insights, leaders can cultivate reciprocal relationships that thrive on mutual respect and cooperation. Emotional connection, another vital component of persuasion, involves tapping into the core concerns and values of individuals. By relating on an emotional level, the persuasiveness of the message is amplified, making it resonate more profoundly with those it seeks to engage. This goes beyond mere emotional manipulation, focusing instead on aligning with genuine values and concerns to forge authentic connections. Narratives or anecdotes that connect emotionally can bridge psychological divides, fostering empathy and understanding that makes the message more compelling.

Credibility, the unwavering foundation of effective persuasion, is paramount. Without credibility, even the most eloquently articulated arguments can lose impact and persuasion falls flat. Establishing credibility involves consistently showcasing competence, integrity, and reliability through actions and words. Sharing personal success stories can lend authenticity, illustrating how concepts and ideas manifest in real-world situations. Moreover, testimonials from peers, clients, or stakeholders bolster credibility by providing third-party validation, reinforcing the perceived expertise. Beyond personal accounts, positioning oneself as a thought leader offers another channel to enhance credibility. Through contributing insightful articles, speaking at conferences, or engaging in meaningful industry discourse, leaders solidify their position as knowledgeable authorities within their realms. This visibility not only enhances influence but also engenders trust, prompting others to seek guidance from and align with those recognized as experts.

Crafting a persuasive communication style entails conveying messages that resonate profoundly with diverse audiences. Clarity and conviction must guide this process; a straightforward yet passionate delivery is crucial. Careful comprehension of audience dynamics allows for the tailoring of communication styles, ensuring resonance across varied settings. The recognition that diverse audiences have distinct needs and preferences empowers leaders to adjust their tonal delivery, language, or presentation style to better align with specific expectations. This adaptive communication approach enhances persuasion and illustrates empathy and understanding, as it reflects consideration for audience diversity and unique perspectives.

Non-verbal cues significantly influence the efficacy of persuasive communication. Factors such as body language, eye contact, and facial expressions contribute to the conveyance of messages beyond verbal articulation. Open gestures, consistent eye contact, and a welcoming demeanor underscore verbal communication, reinforcing trust with the audience. Active listening, an equally essential component of persuasive engagement, conveys genuine interest in understanding others' viewpoints. By listening attentively and responding thoughtfully, leaders demonstrate respect and encourage collaborative dialogue, facilitating easier persuasion by including others in the decision-making process and avoiding unilateral dictate.

These elements, credibility, emotional engagement, and custom-tailored messaging, synergize to craft a persuasive communication style that operates on varying levels. For leaders, honing these skills is empowering, equipping them not just to sway decisions but to actively galvanize action and spearhead significant transformations within teams and organizations. Striking a balance between persuasion and integrity guarantees that influence is wielded in a positive, constructive manner.

In the dynamic interplay of words and deeds, persuasion emerges as an exquisite art form, one that harmonizes logic with emotion, authority with humility, to engender lasting influence and catalyze collective achievements.

USING DIGITAL COMMUNICATION TOOLS EFFECTIVELY

In today's fast-paced world where communication occurs at an unprecedented speed, digital communication tools have become indispensable for effective leadership. These tools serve as the backbone for seamless collaboration and efficient communication, effectively breaking down geographical barriers and enabling teams situated in distant locales, even across continents, to connect in ways that weren't possible just a few decades ago. Whether you're in a position of leadership over a remote team scattered across multiple time zones or are responsible for coordinating an intricate project brimming with complexity and involving partners worldwide, a robust understanding of how these tools function and the role they play is absolutely crucial. Platforms such as Zoom, Microsoft Teams, and Slack have revolutionized the methods by which we communicate, offering a suite of features that facilitate not only meetings and discussions but real-time collaborations as well. These tools do much more than just streamline processes; they significantly enhance productivity while simultaneously fostering a sense of unity and cohesion among team members who might never have the opportunity or privilege to meet face-to-face.

To further elaborate, maintaining a high degree of professionalism in digital interactions is an imperative that cannot be overstressed. Email, which has stood the test of time as a staple of business communication, is all too often misused or underutilized to its full potential. Crafting clear, concise messages is of paramount importance. It's essential to ensure that your subject lines are sufficiently descriptive and your content is structured logically, thereby preventing costly misunderstandings and promoting clear communication. When discussing multiple points, the use of bullet points or numbered lists can significantly enhance clarity. Furthermore, when managing virtual meetings, preparation is key to ensuring that these engagements are effective and productive. Setting clear agendas and sharing them in advance helps keep discussions focused and productive, allowing everyone involved to prepare appropriately. During meetings, make a concerted effort to encourage participation by inviting input from those quieter team members who might not naturally speak up, ensuring that everyone feels included and has a voice in the conversation.

Social media, with its expansive reach, presents both opportunities and challenges for leadership communication in today's digital age. Platforms like LinkedIn offer a valuable space to build and nurture a professional brand, providing a stage to showcase achievements and share insightful industry knowledge. Engaging with online communities through these platforms allows you to connect with peers, enthusiasts, and industry veterans alike, exchanging ideas and staying updated on the latest trends and developments. However, navigating these platforms requires a thoughtful and discerning approach. It is crucial to be mindful of the content you choose to share; it should always reflect your personal values and align with your desired professional image. Engaging authentically with your followers is also important; responding to comments and messages not only builds meaningful relationships but also fosters a sense of community.

To take your virtual communication skills to the next level, consider employing collaboration tools such as Trello or Slack. Trello's visual boards are an excellent tool for project management, enabling effective task organization and comprehensive progress tracking. This allows teams to collaborate on projects seamlessly from inception to completion. Slack, on the other hand, offers real-time messaging and integrates with a myriad of other applications, facilitating seamless and transparent communication within teams, thereby enhancing workflow and productivity. For virtual presentations, tools like Prezi or Canva can significantly elevate your slides. They provide dynamic visuals that capture attention and convey messages more effectively, ensuring your presentations are both engaging and informative.

Interactive Element: Digital Communication Self-Assessment

Take a moment to pause and engage in a reflective exercise to evaluate your current use of digital communication tools. Are there platforms that you might be underutilizing and could integrate more effectively into your regular workflow? Identify one new tool or feature that you could explore further this week, and consider how it might serve to improve your communication efficiency and overall effectiveness.

These digital tools are more than mere conveniences; they are vital components of modern leadership strategies. When leveraged strategically, they can enhance your ability to lead with clarity, precision, and impact in an increasingly connected and fast-paced world. The ability to deftly navigate digital communication platforms and tools stands as a testament to adaptive leadership, empowering individuals to thrive in a dynamic environment while accomplishing collective goals.

BUILDING RAPPORT AND TRUST IN TEAMS

Rapport within the dynamics of team environments is fundamentally the adhesive that cohesively brings individuals together and cements the group, crafting an atmosphere where collaboration is not only possible but flourishes abundantly. It's an essence that transcends mere congenial interactions; it's about etching significant connections that act as conduits for improved trust and synergistic cooperation. When each member of the team feels both understood and appreciated, the entire team transforms into a united front, a cohesive whole that works tirelessly towards a shared vision and common objectives with invigorated enthusiasm. This productive state not only bolsters morale but also serves as a catalyst for innovation and creativity, as team members feel secure and empowered to voice their ideas and undertake calculated risks. Ultimately, rapport is the bedrock upon which trust is constructed, nurturing an environment where collaboration becomes as seamless and natural as breathing, and where obstacles are perceived as challenges to be collectively addressed rather than burdens to be shouldered alone.

To foster trust effectively within the dynamic of teams, it is essential to prioritize one of the most fundamental yet potent tools, active listening. This practice requires not just hearing words but providing undivided attention and thoughtful consideration to what is being communicated. By truly listening, you signal to team members that their opinions are significant and their voices are respected. This demonstrates mutual respect and opens the gates for candid communication. In addition, responding empathetically reinforces a supportive ethos. Consistency in interactions and communication cannot be overstated. Fulfillment of promises and transparency in actions enhance dependability. Trust thrives when team members know they can rely on your words turning into actions. This dependability acts as the core underpinning of solid team dynamics, infusing members with a sense of security and unity in pursuit of collective endeavors.

Effective communication within teams serves as the key to profound understanding and deeper collaboration. Scheduled team-building activities can significantly boost this communicative spirit by crafting opportunities for team members to intermingle outside of their standard work-based interactions. Such activities could range from casual gatherings, like group lunches, to more meticulously organized workshops that aim to develop specific, relevant skills. They serve to dismantle existing barriers and promote camaraderie and enriched connections. Alongside this, cultivating an environment where open dialogue is paramount is crucial. Establish a setting where feedback, both praise and constructive criticism, flows dynamically and without apprehension of negative repercussions. This ensures members feel free to articulate their thoughts and suggestions with ease, reinforcing that each contribution is valued and respected.

Sustaining positive team relationships over time necessitates thoughtful attention and nurturing. Acknowledging and celebrating achievements acts as a substantial motivator. Recognition of accomplishments, whether monumental or minor, imbues members with a sense of fulfillment and buoyed spirits. Public commendation of individual and team contributions fosters pride and incentivizes sustained effort. Equally crucial is the necessity to address conflicts swiftly and constructively. Allowing issues to fester can breed discontent and ultimately precipitate division within the team. Instead, embrace a problem-solving methodology, focusing resolutely on deriving resolutions that accommodate all parties. This proactive stance arrests minor dissent before it escalates into larger disruptions that could potentially fracture team unity.

Interactive Element: Team Trust Checklist

Create a trust assessment checklist tailored to your specific team's needs, one that allows for measuring the level of trust within the group. Include vital criteria such as openness in communication, reliability of team members, and the degree of mutual respect shared among individuals. Regular reviews and reflections upon this checklist can aid in identifying areas requiring improvement as well as celebrating areas of strength.

In conclusion, the endeavor of building rapport and fortifying trust within a team is a continuous process, one that demands unwavering attention and commitment. These elements are not merely advantageous, they are indispensable to the creation of environments wherein teams can truly prosper. As trust emboldens, so too does the potential for pioneering ideas and enduring success, laying down a robust foundation for the advancement and growth that lie ahead.

As we bring this chapter to a close, it bears remembering that effective communication coupled with profound trust is elemental to impactful leadership. These elements sculpt the framework not only for our interactions within teams but also influence the outcomes we drive and the change we catalyze. As we look forward, our subsequent chapter will delve into decision-making strategies, enhancing your leadership acumen with clarity and purpose, allowing you to adeptly navigate through the intricate challenges of leadership.

11

WORK-LIFE INTEGRATION STRATEGIES

UNDERSTANDING WORK-LIFE INTEGRATION VS. BALANCE

It's a Tuesday afternoon, and you're in the middle of a critical project deadline. Your phone buzzes, a reminder of your child's school play happening in just an hour. The tug-of-war between work responsibilities and personal commitments is all too familiar. This is where the concepts of work-life integration and work-life balance come into play. While they sound similar, they offer different approaches to managing your professional and personal lives. Work-life balance suggests a neat separation, a set boundary between work hours and personal time, like a clear line in the sand. It's about maintaining distinct boundaries with the hope of achieving equilibrium. Work-life integration, on the other hand, embraces fluidity, blending professional tasks with personal ones (US Chamber of Commerce, 2022).

Integration means answering emails from your home office while keeping an ear out for your kids or taking a mid-afternoon walk to brainstorm ideas. It's about weaving together the strands of work and life into a harmonious tapestry. The benefits? Flexibility and adaptability come naturally when integration is your guiding principle. You can adjust your schedule to fit both professional obligations and personal pleasures without feeling like you're sacrificing one for the other.

However, challenges exist too. The lines can blur quickly, leading to feelings of being always "on." You might find yourself answering work emails during dinner or having family interruptions during conference calls. For some, this lack of boundaries can be more stressful than beneficial. That's where work-life balance appeals, offering structured boundaries that can provide a sense of stability and predictability, like knowing when you shut down your laptop for the day, it's truly time to unwind.

The key is understanding what suits your lifestyle and career stage best. Maybe you're at a point where integration works beautifully because it allows you to attend midday yoga classes or pick up your children from school without guilt. Or perhaps balance is what you crave, providing a sense of order in a chaotic world. Both approaches have their place, and neither is inherently better than the other.

Let's explore some ways to make integration work effectively, starting with models that have been successful for others. The flexible work schedule model allows you to set your hours based on productivity peaks rather than conventional office timings. It can be a game-changer for those who find inspiration at odd hours or need to accommodate family commitments throughout the day.

The Results-Oriented Work Environment (ROWE) model takes this a step further by focusing solely on outcomes rather than hours worked. In this setup, you're judged by what you achieve, not how long you sit at your desk. It's liberating, especially for those who thrive on autonomy and can self-manage effectively.

Personalization is crucial in making any integration strategy successful. Your needs will differ depending on whether you're an entrepreneur building your brand or a professional navigating a career transition. Family dynamics also play a significant role, perhaps you have young children requiring attention or aging parents needing care.

Regular reassessment is essential; what works today might not suit you tomorrow as life circumstances evolve. Take time to evaluate your current strategy, does it align with your goals? Are there areas causing unnecessary stress? Adjust as needed without guilt; flexibility is about finding what fits now, not forever.

Interactive Element: Integration Assessment Exercise

Consider setting aside time weekly to reflect on your integration strategy's effectiveness. Create a journal entry answering these questions: What worked well this week in balancing work and life? Where did challenges arise? What is one small change I can implement next week to improve integration? This practice fosters awareness and helps tailor your approach to current needs.

The beauty of work-life integration lies in its adaptability; it's an evolving dance between priorities where you get to lead, not follow rigid rules. Embrace this fluidity with confidence and creativity, then your unique rhythm will emerge naturally over time.

TECHNIQUES FOR MANAGING STRESS AND PREVENTING BURNOUT

In the high-stakes realm of leadership, stress often lurks in the background, ready to pounce as you juggle the multifaceted demands of your role. As a leader, one finds oneself constantly navigating through a whirlwind of decision-making, where each choice can feel like a pivotal move, potentially changing the course of events significantly. This pressure cooker environment can quickly become overwhelming, particularly when the immense responsibility of balancing your diverse roles, be it as a leader, mentor, or family member, compounds the already heavy burden. Such scenarios are not just stressful; they can significantly impact your overall well-being if left unchecked. Recognizing these stressors is the crucial first step toward managing them effectively, allowing you to maintain a healthy equilibrium in your personal and professional life.

Mindfulness meditation offers a powerful antidote to this chaos. By concentrating intently on the present moment, you can calm your mind and reduce anxiety substantially. Imagine taking a few quiet moments each day to close your eyes, breathe deeply, and allow your thoughts to settle like serene leaves drifting on a tranquil pond. This practice not only alleviates stress but also enhances your clarity and focus, equipping you to tackle challenges with renewed vigor and energy. Time management techniques, such as the well-regarded Pomodoro Technique, can also be transformative. Breaking your work into manageable intervals with short, restorative breaks can dramatically boost productivity and prevent burnout. The method is simple: you work on a task for 25 minutes, take a brief five-minute respite, and then repeat. It's a straightforward yet highly effective approach that helps maintain concentration and sustain energy throughout the day.

The concept of self-care has rightly gained significant traction and for a good reason. It's a critical component of preventing burnout. Establishing daily self-care rituals can help maintain your energy and overall well-being. Whether it's savoring a quiet cup of tea in the morning, calmly preparing for the day ahead, or unwinding with a captivating book at night, these moments are invaluable. They serve as gentle reminders that you are more than the sum of your to-do list. Physical activity is another cornerstone of self-care. Incorporating even short bursts of exercise into your day can do wonders for both your mood and energy levels. Perhaps a brisk walk during lunch breaks or a quick, rejuvenating yoga session can invigorate your body and mind, providing a much-needed respite from the pressures of the day's demands.

Building resilience against stress is akin to fortifying your defenses, ensuring they are strong and ready before the storm hits. Cognitive-behavioral techniques can play a pivotal role here. By diligently challenging negative thought patterns and reframing challenges as opportunities for growth and learning, you can significantly reduce stress levels. For instance, when faced with a setback, rather than thinking, "I failed," try reframing it as "This is a valuable opportunity to learn and improve." This shift in perspective not only reduces stress but also fosters a growth mindset, essential for leaders who must continually adapt and evolve in a dynamic environment.

Creating a support network is equally vital in managing stress and preventing burnout. Surround yourself with individuals who understand your challenges and can offer emotional support and encouragement. Whether it's your colleagues who can empathize with work-related issues or friends who provide a listening ear during tough times, these connections can serve as vital lifelines. They remind you that you're not alone in this journey, offering fresh perspectives and solutions that you might not have considered otherwise.

Interactive Element: Stress Management Reflection Exercise

Take a moment to list three common sources of stress in your leadership role. Reflect on how these stressors affect your well-being and productivity. Next, identify one mindfulness practice and one time management technique you're interested in trying out this week. Note down how you plan to thoughtfully integrate them into your daily routine.

Remember, stress management isn't about completely eliminating stress, it's about developing and implementing strategies that make it manageable. By proactively addressing stressors and incorporating consistent self-care into your life, you create an environment where burnout stands no chance. Making small, deliberate, yet consistent changes can lead to significant improvements in your overall well-being, empowering you to lead with greater confidence, clarity, and resilience.

CREATING BOUNDARIES THAT PROTECT PERSONAL TIME

Setting boundaries in the whirlwind of today's professional demands isn't just a nice-to-have; it's an undeniable, indispensable necessity. Imagine your personal time not as something you hastily squeeze into your day, sandwiched between meetings and errands, but as sacred moments that demand protection with reverence and intention. By establishing firm and thoughtful boundaries, you create a dedicated sanctuary, carving out indispensable space for personal interests, which might include hobbies like painting, cycling, or gardening that bring you joy and relaxation. Additionally, it's about nurturing relationships, whether that's with family, friends, or even yourself, and allowing yourself the liberty to simply pause, breathe, and be present. These boundaries act as a crucial buffer, a protective force field against work's inevitable and often relentless intrusions, ensuring that when you're off the clock, you can genuinely and wholeheartedly experience life outside of the constant buzz of emails and pressing deadlines.

Communicating these boundaries is equally, if not more, crucial than the boundaries themselves. It's about more than just saying "no" with a resolute tone; it's about clearly and respectfully defining what is acceptable and what is not, setting a transparent framework for mutual understanding. Consider the role of technology in your life and how it can be used judiciously to your advantage. By setting specific times when work notifications are silenced, you allow yourself the focus needed for personal moments without being pulled away by the constant ping of a new message that demands immediate attention. At home, create "no work" zones, areas where your digital devices remain closed, and your attention is entirely, honestly present and available to those around you. This intentional practice not only aids you in unwinding effectively but also sends a clear message to others that your personal time is sacrosanct and non-negotiable.

Naturally, maintaining these boundaries isn't always smooth sailing amidst the unpredictable waves of work. Colleagues or supervisors might occasionally, perhaps unknowingly, overstep, challenging the firm limits you've diligently set. It can be challenging to reinforce them without feeling like you're letting someone down or disappointing a team. This requires a delicate, artful balance of firmness and diplomacy, conveying your stance with clarity and tact. When a boundary is encroached upon, address it promptly and without ambiguity. A straightforward and considerate statement like, "I appreciate the urgency, but I need to adhere to our agreed hours," can reinforce your stance without causing unnecessary friction or misunderstanding.

Tools can serve as beneficial allies in evaluating and fine-tuning your boundaries over time. Consider utilizing boundary assessment worksheets to regularly review your current setup and arrangements. Are they effective? Do they align harmoniously with your evolving priorities? Such reflective exercises provide insightful revelations into whether your boundaries need recalibration and tweaking. For instance, if you find certain restrictions have become too rigid or prove ineffective, adjustments can be made to fit evolving needs and realities.

Recognize that boundary setting isn't a static process with a fixed endpoint; it's a dynamic, ever-evolving journey that changes as you do. It's about discovering and refining what works best for you and being flexible enough to adapt when necessary. A reflection exercise might involve journaling instances where boundaries felt tested or challenged and brainstorming creative solutions and strategies to effectively reinforce them. This ongoing dialogue with yourself ensures that your personal time remains protected, cherished, and valued as it should be.

Ultimately, boundaries empower you to engage fully and meaningfully in both work and life. They provide you with the freedom and permission to be present in each moment, whether you're deeply immersed in tackling an important project deadline or savoring a quiet, heartfelt dinner with loved ones. By valuing your time and setting clear, respectful expectations with others, you cultivate a balanced rhythm and harmony that respects your professional aspirations and personal well-being alike.

Creating these boundaries isn't about isolating parts of your life into disparate segments; it's about integrating them in a purposeful way that honors who you are and what you need both now and moving forward. When done thoughtfully and intentionally, boundaries become less of a barrier and more of a bridge that connects you to what truly matters most, allowing you to navigate the complex demands of modern life with an elegance and confidence that reflects your most authentic self.

INTEGRATING PERSONAL WELL-BEING INTO LEADERSHIP

Your well-being is more than just a personal matter, it's in fact the cornerstone of effective leadership. When you feel well, both physically and mentally, your ability to make sound decisions improves remarkably. This isn't just about getting enough sleep or eating right, although those are crucial. It's about nurturing yourself to the point where clarity becomes your default setting, when facing a challenging decision, one that requires not only logic but also empathy and insight. If you're running on fumes, it's like trying to see through fog. But when you're well-rested and centered, that fog lifts, revealing a clear path ahead.

Empathy, too, flourishes when you're grounded in well-being. As a leader, understanding and connecting with your team is vital. When you're at your best, you can genuinely listen to others, read between the lines of what's said, and respond with compassion and insight. This empathetic approach not only strengthens relationships but also fosters a more collaborative environment. Your team feels heard and valued, which can lead to increased morale and productivity.

So, how do you prioritize this well-being amid a hectic schedule? Start with small, intentional practices that fit seamlessly into your routine. Scheduling regular wellness breaks can be a game-changer. These aren't long vacations but brief intermissions; a quick walk around the block or a few minutes of deep breathing that refresh your mind and body. Gratitude practices can be equally transformative. Taking a moment each day to reflect on what you're thankful for can shift your mindset from one of stress to appreciation. This simple act can have profound effects on your outlook and leadership style.

The ripple effect of prioritizing well-being extends beyond personal benefits; it influences the entire organizational culture. When you lead by example, prioritizing your health and happiness, it sets a tone for the workplace. Your team observes your actions and feels encouraged to follow suit, creating a ripple effect that promotes a culture of well-being. This shift can lead to reduced burnout rates, increased job satisfaction, and a more engaged workforce.

To support this ongoing commitment to personal well-being, practical tools can be invaluable. Well-being trackers are a great resource, they help you monitor habits and progress over time, providing tangible insights into what's working and what needs adjustment. Similarly, journals dedicated to tracking mood and energy levels can offer clarity on how certain activities or routines impact your overall wellness.

Don't underestimate the power of community support in this journey. Accessing wellness resources and support networks can provide encouragement and accountability. Whether it's joining a meditation group or participating in wellness workshops, these connections reinforce your commitment to well-being. They remind you that you're not alone in this pursuit.

Textual Element: Well-being Checklist

Consider creating a checklist of daily well-being practices tailored to your needs. Include activities like morning stretches, hydration reminders, gratitude reflections, and designated screen-free times. This checklist serves as a gentle nudge toward maintaining balance amidst the demands of leadership.

As we wrap up this exploration of integrating personal well-being into leadership, remember that taking care of yourself isn't selfish, it's essential for showing up as your best self in all areas of life. By prioritizing well-being, you not only enhance your effectiveness as a leader but also inspire those around you to do the same.

In embracing these strategies for well-being, you lay the foundation for lasting impact, not just in your own life but in the lives of those you lead. As we move forward to explore the next chapter on decision-making and delegation strategies, keep in mind that nurturing yourself is the first step towards empowering others effectively.

12

INSPIRING ACTION AND LEADING WITH PURPOSE

CULTIVATING A GROWTH MINDSET FOR LEADERSHIP

Let me take you back to a moment that changed everything for me. I was standing at a crossroads, facing a project riddled with challenges that seemed utterly insurmountable and daunting. My team was discouraged, and the path forward was anything but clear. It was during this period of uncertainty that I stumbled upon the concept of a growth mindset, a concept introduced by renowned psychologist Carol Dweck. A growth mindset is the belief that abilities and intelligence are not fixed traits but can be nurtured and developed through dedication, commitment, and rigorous hard work. This philosophy sharply contrasts with a fixed mindset, a perspective where individuals perceive their talents as static, unchangeable traits, much like a painting set in stone.

Understanding this difference is crucial in leadership, as it shapes how we approach not only challenges but opportunities as well, and how we perceive, embrace, or constrain our potential.

Embracing a growth mindset means shifting our perspective to see every obstacle as a hidden opportunity to learn and grow, rather than as an insurmountable barrier to success.

Developing a growth mindset requires intentional engagement in strategic techniques. It begins with the crucial process of reframing setbacks, viewing them not as personal failings but as valuable, indispensable feedback. Instead of perceiving failures as devastating personal shortcomings, they should be considered stepping stones on your path to improvement and personal development. This mental shift fosters not only resilience but also encourages you to embrace challenges with open arms. Imagine, if you will, a scenario where a pivotal presentation didn't unfold as planned. Rather than fixating endlessly on what went wrong, use it as a learning tool by analyzing all possible facets of what could be improved for the next opportunity. This reflection not only builds your skills but also fuels your confidence for future endeavors, emboldening you every step of the way.

One of the most transformative aspects of a growth mindset is its profound impact on leadership effectiveness. When you embrace and cultivate a growth-oriented approach, you inherently create a fertile ground for innovation and boundless creativity within your team. You're more inclined to encourage experimentation, comfortable in the knowledge that mistakes are simply part of the natural learning process. This mindset nurtures an environment where team members feel safe to share ideas freely, leading to an influx of fresh, innovative solutions and continuous improvement. A leader with a growth mindset inspires adaptability within their team, enabling them to navigate and embrace change with agility, grace, and utmost confidence.

To effectively promote a growth mindset within your team, focus on developing an atmosphere that encourages open dialogue about mistakes and shortcomings. Create a culture where discussing failures is not merely accepted but is instead valued as essential learning moments. Celebrate and commend effort and learning over innate talent, acknowledging that dedication and perseverance are the true key ingredients to success. By shifting the focus from solely achieving perfect results to valuing the expansive journey of growth, you empower your team to take calculated risks, pursue excellence with passion, and innovate fearlessly.

Interactive Element: Growth Mindset Reflection Exercise

Take this moment to engage deeply and reflect on a recent challenge you faced in your professional life. Write down how you initially perceived the seemingly insurmountable obstacle and consider ways you could reframe it as a potential opportunity for learning and growth. Consider the invaluable lessons you gleaned from the experience and how it has pulsed your growth journey forward.

The benefits of cultivating a growth mindset extend far beyond the realm of individual development; they permeate the very fabric of team dynamics and organizational culture. When leaders model and exemplify this mindset, it becomes contagious, inspiring others within the organization to adopt a similar progressive approach. In turn, this fosters a culture of continuous improvement where innovation thrives, and challenges are met with enthusiasm and vigor rather than resistance and reluctance.

By nurturing a growth mindset in your leadership, you're not only enhancing your personal effectiveness and transformational leadership capabilities but also creating an environment ripe for your team's flourishing. As you embrace challenges as pivotal opportunities for learning and encourage your team to do the same, you'll witness a transformative evolution in how they approach their work, fueled by creativity, adaptability, and an unwavering, collective commitment to growth. Every setback is a setup for a grand comeback.

INSPIRING AND MOTIVATING YOUR TEAM

Imagine walking into a room buzzing with energy, where everyone knows exactly why they are there and what they're striving for. That's the power of a compelling vision. Crafting a shared team vision is about painting a vivid picture of the future that everyone can see and feel. It's not just about goals or targets; it's about the bigger picture, what the team stands for, and what they aspire to achieve together. Communicating this vision with passion and clarity is crucial. Your enthusiasm and belief in the vision can ignite the same excitement within your team, motivating them to contribute their best efforts. When you speak about this vision, let your words paint images in their minds, allowing them to envision their role in bringing this vision to life.

Recognizing and rewarding team efforts is a critical aspect of maintaining motivation. Implementing recognition programs can transform the way your team feels about their work. Whether it's a formal monthly award or just a shout-out during meetings, acknowledging contributions can lift spirits and reinforce positive behaviors. Personalized appreciation methods, such as handwritten notes or tailored rewards that align with individual preferences, make recognition feel genuine and meaningful. These gestures show that you see and value their hard work, fostering a culture of appreciation. Remember, it's not always about grand gestures; sometimes, a sincere "thank you" at the right moment can make all the difference.

Empowerment is another cornerstone of motivation. When team members feel empowered, they're more engaged and invested in their work. Delegating meaningful responsibilities shows your trust in their capabilities, encouraging them to take ownership of projects. This sense of ownership is a powerful motivator, driving them to excel and innovate. Encouraging autonomy and initiative further boosts motivation, allowing team members to explore their strengths and creativity. By giving them the freedom to experiment and make decisions, you foster an environment where innovation thrives. It's about creating a space where they feel safe to take risks and learn from outcomes.

Building a motivating work environment goes beyond individual recognition; it's about fostering a culture where everyone feels inspired to contribute. Collaboration and teamwork should be at the heart of this environment. Encourage open communication and create opportunities for team members to work together on projects that challenge them and stimulate creativity. By fostering a collaborative atmosphere, you tap into the collective intelligence of the group, leading to innovative solutions and stronger team bonds. Providing opportunities for professional growth and development is equally important. Whether through workshops, training sessions, or mentorship programs, investing in your team's growth shows that you care about their future as much as their present contributions.

An inspiring work culture thrives on mutual respect and shared values. Encourage team members to share ideas openly, without fear of judgment. Celebrate diversity in thought, background, and approach, as these differences can lead to richer discussions and more creative outcomes. Acknowledge that each member brings unique strengths to the table, and leverage these strengths to achieve common goals. Create rituals or traditions that reinforce these values, whether it's weekly brainstorming sessions or monthly team outings, to strengthen the sense of community.

As you cultivate this environment, remember that leadership is not just about directing but also about listening and adapting. Stay attuned to the needs and aspirations of your team, adjusting your approach as necessary to maintain alignment with their evolving goals. This adaptability not only enhances your leadership effectiveness but also empowers your team to take initiative and thrive in a supportive environment.

Inspiring action within your team requires more than just words, it demands genuine commitment to creating an environment where everyone feels valued and motivated to contribute their best. Each step you take toward building this culture strengthens your team's foundation, enabling them to reach new heights together. Motivation is not a one-time effort but an ongoing process that evolves with the team. As you lead with purpose and passion, let these principles guide you in fostering a dynamic and motivated team ready to achieve great things together.

LEADING WITH AUTHENTICITY AND INTEGRITY

Leading authentically encompasses embodying your true self, genuinely and without any pretense. It's an embodiment of remaining steadfast to your inherent principles, even amidst external pressures to conform, which can feel daunting and overwhelming. Authentic leadership is firmly anchored in the virtues of transparency and honesty, which are indispensable pillars in the edifice of trust-building. When leaders approach leadership with an open mind and heart, their team gains clarity on their intentions, fostering an environment steeped in openness and candor. Individuals tend to gravitate toward those leaders who exhibit genuineness, those who candidly express both their vulnerabilities and strengths with unvarnished honesty. Followers understand your core values and what to anticipate, establishing a foundation for enduring loyalty and profound respect. This methodology bolsters not only leadership but also cultivates a safe space where team members feel liberated to bring forth their authentic selves.

Trust and loyalty naturally burgeon from authenticity in leadership. When team members perceive genuineness in their leaders, they are more inclined to trust and remain loyal. Take for instance, figures like Oprah Winfrey, whose authenticity has elevated her to iconic status, transcending just the media and penetrating leadership realms globally. Her openness concerning personal struggles and monumental triumphs reverberates deeply with the masses, forging a steadfast following that places unwavering trust in her vision and leadership. Engendering such deep-rooted trust within a team transcends mere openness; it necessitates crafting channels for candid communication and constructive feedback. Leaders should encourage team members to express their thoughts openly and without fear of judgment. Techniques such as regular check-ins and implementing open-door policies are instrumental in nurturing this atmosphere, laying a robust groundwork of trust that propels team cohesion and loyalty.

Maintaining integrity in leadership is fundamentally about ensuring your deeds align with your ethical convictions, even when confronted with arduous decisions. It's about making choices that are not only beneficial in the immediate context but also harmonious with your enduring values and principles. Accountability in one's actions forms a foundational stone of integrity. This involves acknowledging any mistakes and owning up rather than shifting blame elsewhere. By doing so, leaders set a compelling example for their teams, showcasing that integrity transcends grand gestures and finds expression even in the everyday decisions that define our leadership personas. Through consistently aligning decisions with personal values, a leader earns their team's reliance on their judgment, thereby reinforcing trust and respect within the team dynamics.

Self-reflection is an imperative and indispensable apparatus for leaders who aspire to authenticity. Routinely evaluating your leadership style and its effectiveness is crucial in maintaining alignment with core values while adapting to evolving circumstances. Such introspection enables identification of zones where one might have deviated from central beliefs or where external pressures might have swayed decision-making processes. Seeking feedback from colleagues and team members provides invaluable external perspectives on how leadership is being perceived and highlights areas for potential improvement. Engaging in this process not only fuels personal growth but also signals a commitment to self-improvement and authenticity. By embracing feedback openly, leaders illustrate to their teams that growth and improvement are perpetual processes, reinforcing a culture rooted in authenticity within their organization.

Regular self-assessment exercises prove remarkably enlightening. Allocate time monthly to deliberate on recent decisions and interactions. Ponder questions such as: Did this decision align with my values? How adeptly did I manage feedback or conflict? What areas possess room for improvement? This practice anchors you firmly in your principles, enabling you to navigate leadership hurdles with unwavering integrity and authenticity. It's crucial to seek out diverse viewpoints. Solicit input from those who might have differing perspectives. This diversity can unearth hidden blind spots and encourage a more inclusive, comprehensive leadership approach.

The journey of authentic leadership is one of perpetual growth, where each stride toward heightened self-awareness nurtures more profound connections with those you lead. By anchoring your leadership in authenticity and integrity, you foster an environment where trust naturally propagates, creativity knows no bounds, and teams coalesce under unified values.

SUSTAINING PURPOSE-DRIVEN LEADERSHIP: AN IN-DEPTH EXPLORATION

Leading with a well-defined purpose is akin to possessing a steadfast compass, artfully guiding you through the multifaceted challenges and intricacies inherent in leadership roles. It's about harmonizing what you endeavor with who you inherently are, at the very core of your being. When leadership aspirations are intimately intertwined with personal purpose, the ensuing impact is not only profound but also remarkably transformational. This profound alignment enhances both your efficacy as a leader and your individual sense of fulfillment and satisfaction. Purpose acts as a powerful motivator, an intrinsic driving force that propels you diligently forward, resilient even in the face of daunting and formidable obstacles. It provides both clarity and unmistakable direction, ensuring that every decision you undertake aligns seamlessly with your overarching long-term vision. This alignment doesn't merely amplify your leadership capabilities; it renders the entire journey significantly more gratifying, cultivating a deep sense of meaning and accomplishment that energizes sustainable success over the long term.

The Role of a Purpose Statement in Leadership

Articulating your purpose with clarity and precision is an indispensable aspect of this transformative journey. It begins with the thoughtful crafting of a purpose statement, a written reflection of what genuinely inspires and drives you, alongside an explanation of why this drive is of significant importance. This statement serves as your guiding light, a metaphorical north star, continually reminding you of the broader picture, even amid the most challenging day-to-day tasks and encounters. However, merely having this purpose silently inscribed or noted down is insufficient; it must be communicated with clarity and consistency through your actions, intentions, and spoken words. Your team should not only observe but also deeply feel your purpose permeating every aspect of what you do, from your approach and strategy in meetings to the grace and resilience with which you handle unforeseen setbacks. This unwavering consistency fosters trust and inspires others around you, rallying them around shared values and collective goals.

Creating a Culture of Purpose

Purpose-driven leadership extends beyond individual alignment; it radiates outward, actively shaping the fundamental culture and ethos of your entire organization. A distinct and compelling purpose can fundamentally transform a company's cultural dynamics, fostering an environment where every team member genuinely feels a part of something vastly larger than themselves. Within such a culture, meaning and motivation become intrinsically linked, naturally driving higher levels of engagement, performance, and innovation. When organizational objectives are closely aligned with a well-articulated purpose, teams work collaboratively with a united, singular spirit, cohesively striving to achieve meaningful and impactful outcomes.

Reflections and Celebrations in Purposeful Leadership

Sustaining such a purpose over an extended period necessitates regular and thoughtful reflection. Revisit your purpose statement periodically, refine it as you evolve, and adapt it as circumstances change and unfold. This ensures that your leadership remains both relevant and impactful, skillfully adapting to new challenges while remaining staunchly true to core and foundational values. Celebrating achievements that resonate with your purpose underscores its significance, creating meaningful milestones that mark progress and inspire continued commitment and engagement. These celebratory moments need not always be grandiose; often, acknowledging smaller victories and appreciating the lessons learned during the journey can be equally powerful and enlightening.

Continuous Purposeful Leadership in a Dynamic World

In our intricate, ever-evolving world, maintaining purpose-driven leadership demands both intention and diligent attention. It's about staying deeply connected to what genuinely matters and allowing that connection to guide your actions with purpose every single day. As you continue on your path to lead with purpose, recognize that you are not just guiding a team or managing an organization, you're building and contributing to a significant legacy of meaningful impact that transcends far beyond immediate and short-term results.

As we conclude this chapter, remember that sustaining purpose-driven leadership is far from a one-time endeavor. It is instead an enduring practice that brings enrichment to every facet of your leadership journey. It's about perpetually aligning your actions with your foundational values and celebrating the myriad milestones reflecting purposeful growth.

CONCLUSION

As we close this journey together, let's take a moment to reflect on the heart of this book, empowering you to communicate effectively and lead with confidence aligned to your true self. Throughout these chapters, we've navigated the complexities of leadership, explored the depths of self-awareness, and uncovered strategies that empower you to step into your full potential.

We began by delving into the foundations of authentic confidence, emphasizing that leadership is not about fitting into a mold but embracing your unique strengths. From understanding your leadership style to overcoming self-doubt, the path to confidence is paved with self-awareness and authenticity. We've tackled the barriers that often prevent women from being heard, offering techniques to communicate assertively and effectively, without compromising who you are.

In exploring mentorship and networking, we recognized the power of connection. Building a support system and engaging with mentors can transform your career trajectory, offering insights and opportunities you might not have envisioned alone.

We've examined the importance of navigating gender bias and workplace challenges, equipping you with strategies to gain visibility and recognition in your field.

As you balanced professional ambitions with personal life, you discovered how to set boundaries that protect your time and energy. By crafting your personal brand, you learned to showcase your strengths and align your professional identity with your values. We also delved into emotional intelligence and self-awareness, key aspects that enhance your leadership effectiveness and foster strong team dynamics.

No journey of leadership is without its setbacks. Building resilience and adaptability equips you to bounce back stronger, turning challenges into growth opportunities. We've seen how inclusive leadership and diversity drive innovation, highlighting the importance of embracing varied perspectives in your team. Leading with empathy and understanding, you create an environment where everyone feels valued and inspired to contribute their best.

As you set goals and craft your personal vision, remember that leadership is as much about inspiring yourself as it is about inspiring others. Your journey is unique, and your vision serves as a guiding light, influencing your decisions and actions. Embrace the power of communication to amplify your impact, whether through public speaking or digital platforms. Building rapport and trust within your team fosters collaboration and propels collective success.

The work-life integration strategies we discussed remind you that leadership encompasses all aspects of life. Balancing professional commitments with personal well-being is crucial to sustaining your energy and passion. Remember that leading with authenticity and integrity inspires those around you to do the same, creating a ripple effect of positive change.

Now, it's your turn to reflect on these insights and consider how you can apply them to your own journey. What steps will you take to implement these strategies in your leadership approach? How can you inspire others by sharing your story and experiences? Your voice and perspective hold incredible power, and I encourage you to embrace your leadership potential fully.

We at FREEDOM PUBLICATIONS are deeply grateful for your trust and engagement throughout this book. Thank you for allowing us to be a part of your growth journey. Your willingness to explore these ideas and apply them to your life is a testament to your commitment to becoming the leader you are meant to be.

As you move forward, we invite you to stay connected. Share your progress, challenges, and triumphs with us and the community of women leaders inspired by the principles in this book. Together, we can continue to support and uplift each other, creating a network of empowerment and encouragement.

Remember, leadership is not a destination but a continuous journey of growth and discovery. Embrace it with confidence, communicate with impact, and lead with purpose. Your influence extends beyond your immediate sphere, inspiring others to do the same. Together, we can make a meaningful difference in our careers, businesses, and lives, leading authentically and inspiring others to follow.

Here's to the remarkable leader you are becoming. Your journey is just beginning, and the possibilities are endless.

UNLOCK THE POWER OF LEADERSHIP

"Leadership is hard to define and good leadership even harder. But if you can get people to follow you to the ends of the earth, you are a great leader."

— *INDRA NOOYI (FORMER CEO OF PEPSICO)*

Your opinion is powerful!

By sharing your thoughts on '**Leadership For Women**', you're not just reflecting on your own journey, you're giving others the courage and inspiration to begin theirs.

If this book has helped you gain a better understanding of your current Leadership skills and your plans for growth and development, your story could be the light that someone else needs to make a change. Every review is a ripple that reaches someone who is ready to grow, succeed and thrive.

Why Your Review Matters:

- **Inspire Others:** Your feedback could be the nudge someone needs to invest in themselves and their future.
- **Share Your Wins:** When you highlight what worked for you, you help others see that success is within their reach.
- **Support the Mission:** Your review spreads the message of the benefits of *Emotional Intelligence* to more people around the world.

How to Write a Review:

1. **Be Honest:** Share your favorite parts, key takeaways, or how the book made a difference in your life.
2. **Keep It Simple:** A few sentences about what you loved is all it takes to make an impact.
3. **Post It Online:** Reviews on Amazon or Goodreads are the best way to help others discover this guide.

We love helping others and hope you will do the same. Thank you!

Freedom Publications: 'Your Partner in Personal Growth and Success'.

Scan the QR code to leave your review:

REFERENCES

Caesar, C. (2024, September 25). *Leadership style assessments: What kind of leader are you? The Predictive Index.* https://www.predictiveindex.com/blog/leadership-style-assessments/

Values-Based Leadership across Difference: The life and legacy of Nelson Mandela. (n.d.). HKS Case Program. https://case.hks.harvard.edu/values-based-leadership-across-difference-the-life-and-legacy-of-nelson-mandela/

Wise, L. (2025, March 19). *6 Ways to build confidence as a woman in business. mba.com.* https://www.mba.com/business-school-and-careers/women-in-business/6-ways-build-confidence-as-woman-business

Thompkins, S. (2025, May 8). *Emotional intelligence and leadership effectiveness: bringing out the best. CCL.* https://www.ccl.org/articles/leading-effectively-articles/emotional-intelligence-and-leadership-effectiveness/

Stressed out? Be assertive. (2024, January 20). Mayo Clinic. https://www.mayoclinic.org/healthy-lifestyle/stress-management/in-depth/assertive/art-20044644

Geller, A. (2025, May 25). *The role of gender in interpersonal communication in the workplace. Connected Speech Pathology.* https://connectedspeechpathology.com/blog/the-role-of-gender-in-interpersonal-communication-in-the-workplace

Sampaio, N. (2025, June 21). *Mastering Executive Presence: 7 Coaching Techniques for Leaders. IMD business school for management and leadership courses.* https://www.imd.org/blog/leadership/executive-presence/

Mills, G. R. (2022, December 5). *Council Post: A simple framework for managing difficult conversations. Forbes.* https://www.forbes.com/councils/forbescoachescouncil/2022/12/05/a-simple-framework-for-managing-difficult-conversations/

Elements of effective practice for mentoring | Enhance your mentoring program. (2025, June 26). MENTOR. https://www.mentoring.org/resource/elements-of-effective-practice-for-mentoring/

Rua-Gomez, C., Carnabuci, G., & Goossen, M. (2024, March 20). *Research: How Women can Build High-Status Networks. Harvard Business Review.* https://hbr.org/2024/03/research-how-women-can-build-high-status-networks

Lahoria, R. (2023, April 28). *How to effectively use LinkedIn for career development.* https://www.linkedin.com/pulse/how-effectively-use-linkedin-career-development-rahul-lahoria

Toxboe, A. (2023, March 23). *Circles of influence. Learning Loop.* https://learningloop.io/glossary/circles-of-influence

Krivkovich, A., Field, E., Yee, L., McConnell, M., & Smith, H. (2024, September 17). *Women in the Workplace 2024: The 10th-anniversary report*. McKinsey & Company. https://www.mckinsey.com/featured-insights/diversity-and-inclusion/women-in-the-workplace

Schnieders, A. (2024, December 19). *Gender bias in the workplace: Spotting It & Tips to fight it*. Chronus. https://chronus.com/blog/how-to-overcome-gender-bias-in-the-workplace

Paulise, L. (2023, March 8). *75% of women executives experience imposter syndrome in the workplace*. Forbes. https://www.forbes.com/sites/lucianapaulise/2023/03/08/75-of-women-executives-experience-imposter-syndrome-in-the-workplace/

Cooks-Campbell, A. (2025, April 29). *12 tips to achieve a healthy work-life balance*. BetterUp. https://www.betterup.com/blog/how-to-have-good-work-life-balance

Arruda, W. (2024, October 2). *How women can use personal branding to accelerate career success*. Forbes. https://www.forbes.com/sites/williamarruda/2024/10/02/how-women-use-personal-branding-for-career-success/

Personal Brand Values: A guide to building an Authentic reputation. (2024, January 16). https://www.brandcredential.com/post/personal-brand-values-a-guide-to-building-an-authentic-reputation

Asare, R. (2023, November 2). *The power of consistency in personal branding*. https://www.linkedin.com/pulse/power-consistency-personal-branding-richmond-asare-g4qnf

Marketing Director. (2025, April 2). *How Women Can Create Visibility in the Workplace - HERC Jobs*. Higher Education Jobs - Higher Education Recruitment Consortium. https://www.hercjobs.org/how-women-can-create-visibility-and-recognition-in-the-workplace/

Thompkins, S. (2025b, May 8). *Emotional intelligence and leadership effectiveness: bringing out the best*. CCL. https://www.ccl.org/articles/leading-effectively-articles/emotional-intelligence-and-leadership-effectiveness/

Freedman, J. (2020, December 2). *Case study: Emotional Intelligence for People-First Leadership at FedEx Express*. Six Seconds. https://www.6seconds.org/2014/01/14/case-study-emotional-intelligence-people-first-leadership-fedex-express/

Milston, S. (2024, April 16). *Empathy Mapping as a Leadership and Culture Tool — The Spark Mill - we make change possible*. The Spark Mill - We Make Change Possible. https://www.thesparkmill.com/blog-posts/empathymappingculturetool

Martin, L. N., & Delgado, M. R. (2011). The Influence of Emotion Regulation on Decision-making under Risk. *Journal of Cognitive Neuroscience, 23*(9), 2569–2581. https://doi.org/10.1162/jocn.2011.21618

Parker, N. S. (2023). The resilience of women leaders [Conference-proceeding]. In Regent University School of Business & Leadership, *Regent Research Roundtables Proceedings* (pp. 242–262). Regent University School of Business & Leadership. https://www.regent.

edu/wp-content/uploads/2023/01/Regent-Research-Roundtables-2023-Organizational-Leadership-Parker.pdf

Thompkins, S. (2025c, May 8). Emotional intelligence and leadership effectiveness: bringing out the best. CCL. https://www.ccl.org/articles/leading-effectively-articles/emotional-intelligence-and-leadership-effectiveness/

Explore 9 diverse leadership styles. (n.d.). https://www.cesarritzcolleges.edu/en/news/leadership-styles/

Mattina, R., & Mattina, R. (2025, July 11). Diversity and inclusion in the workplace: Key benefits, real challenges, and strategies for success. Achievers. https://www.achievers.com/blog/diversity-and-inclusion/

Toguri, T. (2024, August 9). How a diverse workplace can Drive Innovation (Research-Backed). MentorcliQ. https://www.mentorcliq.com/blog/how-a-diverse-workplace-can-drive-innovation

Gentry, B. (2025, June 9). The importance of empathy in the workplace. CCL. https://www.ccl.org/articles/leading-effectively-articles/empathy-in-the-workplace-a-tool-for-effective-leadership/

Advantage, A. T. (2024, November 19). Vision and goal setting. Aurora Training Advantage. https://auroratrainingadvantage.com/leadership/vision-goal-setting-leadership/

Adams, L. (2025, March 16). SMART goals for women: How to achieve what you never thought possible! - Womensoutfront.com. womensoutfront.com. https://womensoutfront.com/smart-goals-for-women/

Create your personal strategic plan. (n.d.). ASAE. https://www.asaecenter.org/association-careerhq/career/articles/career-management/create-your-personal-strategic-plan

Toastmasters International -Public speaking tips. (n.d.). IP. https://www.toastmasters.org/resources/public-speaking-tips

Friedman, R. (2024, January 10). How High-Performing Teams Build Trust. Harvard Business Review. https://hbr.org/2024/01/how-high-performing-teams-build-trust

Fallon-O'Leary, D. (2025, July 11). Work-Life Integration vs. Work-Life Balance. CO- by US Chamber of Commerce. https://www.uschamber.com/co/grow/thrive/work-life-integration-vs-work-life-balance

Njawaya, M. (2024, March 17). Ditch the Drama, Lead with Calm: Powerful Stress Management Strategies for Women Leaders. https://www.linkedin.com/pulse/ditch-drama-lead-calm-powerful-stress-management-women-njawaya-ouxgc

Sanok, J. (2022, April 14). A guide to setting better boundaries. Harvard Business Review. https://hbr.org/2022/04/a-guide-to-setting-better-boundaries

Shane. (2021, February 5). Carol Dweck: A Summary of Growth and Fixed Mindsets. Farnam Street. https://fs.blog/carol-dweck-mindset/

Grossman, D. (2024, October 1). Authentic leadership: what it is, and how to achieve it. https://www.yourthoughtpartner.com/blog/authentic-leadership

Kille, C. (2023, February 22). Council Post: Leading with Purpose and Vision: How to inspire and Motivate your team. Forbes. https://www.forbes.com/councils/forbesbusinesscouncil/2023/02/22/leading-with-purpose-and-vision-how-to-inspire-and-motivate-your-team/

Graham, P., Leslie, J., Gentry, B., & Wormington, S. (2025, May 8). Purpose in leadership: Why & how. CCL. https://www.ccl.org/articles/leading-effectively-articles/purpose-in-leadership-why-how/

ABOUT THE PUBLISHER

Freedom Publications is a respected name in business literature and self-help books, dedicated to providing readers from all walks of life with the tools and insights to succeed in today's competitive and ever-evolving world. Our books cater to teams, leaders, managers, entrepreneurs, professionals, executives, and everyday individuals; young and old, eager to sharpen their skills, elevate their thinking, and make impactful changes in their careers and lives.

Our books are carefully crafted to deliver practical, accessible guidance on everything from building cohesive teams and inspiring effective leadership to boosting productivity and achieving personal and professional goals. With a focus on real-world applications, our books empower readers to turn concepts into actionable strategies that benefit both individuals and groups, enabling stronger communication, smarter decision-making, and sustained success across any field.

Whether you're a business leader striving to lead your team with vision, a professional looking to grow your skill set, an entrepreneur ready to take your venture to the next level, or simply someone interested in improving everyday effectiveness, Freedom Publications is your essential resource for the insights and knowledge to thrive in every aspect of modern business.

Freedom Publications: Your Partner in Personal Growth and Success.